카인의 後裔

The Descendants of Cain

Hwang Sun-wŏn

Translated by
Suh Ji-moon and Julie Pickering

An East Gate Book

M.E. Sharpe/UNESCO Publishing

An East Gate Book

UNESCO COLLECTION OF REPRESENTATIVE WORKS
The publication of this work was assisted by a contribution of the Government
of the Republic of Korea under UNESCO's Funds-in-Trust Programme.

UNESCO ISBN 92-3-103429-4

Copyright © 1997 by Suh Ji-moon and Julie Pickering

Cover photograph : Park Seung-u
Calligraphy : Park Won-kyu

Library of Congress Cataloging-in-Publication Data

Hwang, Sun-wŏn, 1915–
[K'ain ŭi Huye. English]
The descendants of Cain / by Hwang Sun-wŏn ;
translated by Suh Ji-moon and Julie Pickering.
p.   cm.—(UNESCO collection of representative works)
"An East Gate book."
ISBN 0-7656-0136-2 (cloth : alk. paper).—ISBN 0-7656-0137-0 (paper : alk. paper)
I. Title.
PL991.29.S9K313   1997
895.7′33—dc21
97-2564
CIP

Printed in the United States of America

The paper used in this publication meets the minimum requirements of the
American National Standard for Information Sciences—
Permanence of Paper for Printed Library Materials,
ANSI Z 39.48-1984.

BM (c)   10   9   8   7   6   5   4   3   2   1
BM (p)   10   9   8   7   6   5   4   3   2   1

Introduction

Born in 1915 while Korea was under Japanese colonial rule, Hwang Sun-wŏn published his first poem at age sixteen. He published two collections of poems as a student and received a bachelor's degree in English literature from Waseda University in Tokyo. In 1940, a year after graduating and returning to Korea, he published his first collection of short stories. Two years later, Japanese colonial authorities outlawed all publication in Korean. Hwang wrote in private, without any assurance that his writings would ever be published. All the while, he lived in hiding to avoid being pressed into forced labor in Japanese mines or war supply factories.

Beautifully crafted, the stories he wrote in those days of anguish are among the best-loved classics of modern Korean literature. In the bitter circumstances of Korea at that time, Hwang explored the timeless life patterns of ordinary people, lovingly commemorating their dreams, hopes, sorrows, and idiosyncrasies.

Liberation from Japanese colonial rule in August 1945 was a joy to every Korean, but Hwang was soon engulfed in the whirlwind of terror created by the establishment of communist rule in the northern half of the peninsula. His experiences as a landlord's son in a time of land reform and social turmoil form the basis of *The Descendants of Cain*.

Published in 1954 in Seoul, *The Descendants of Cain* (Kain ŭi Huye) was an immediate success and has been a steady best seller ever since. It focuses on a national crisis which changed the course of Korean history and the lives of half the Korean population, vividly depicting the destruction of an old and close-knit society. The traditional Korean way of life remained strong until 1945–46, when the story in the novel unfolds. Tenant farmers, most of whom had tilled the same land over many generations, were bound by multiple ties to the landlords. The farmers were not the legal property of the landowners, but in a country of limited arable land and little mobility, termination of land tenure meant an utterly disastrous fall to the status of vagabond and pariah. Therefore, the tenants could not assert their rights vis-à-vis the landowners. It was also impossible for tenants to escape poverty, as the standard rent throughout the country was half the yield and year after year most farmers had to borrow seed grain from their landlords at fifty percent interest.

On the other hand, because land was scarce, farmers were grateful to be allowed to stay on as tenants. They were also heavily reliant on their landlords for emergency relief, seasonal doles, and so on. Most importantly, peasants accepted their lot as their fate. Having had their lives interwoven with the landlords' family over many generations, their loyalty was almost second nature to them. It is true that Japanese colonial rule weakened the power and authority of the *yangban* class—to which most landowners belonged—by forcing them ultimately to give up even their proud names and adopt Japanese ones. Japan's exploitation of Korea, from 1910 to 1945, which culminated in the massive conscription of manpower and collection of grain and metal goods during World War II, reduced the country to famine and despair. Social structure and social ties were weakened thereby, but the centuries-old relationship between landlord and tenant did not disintegrate entirely until the communists came to power and enforced land reform.

The communists denounced intellectuals as well as landlords because most educated people were from the landowning class, and in traditional Korean society the *yangban* class monopolized power by monopolizing learning. Hun, the central male character of *The Descendants of Cain*, is a typical heir of the Korean landowning class. His utter passivity may seem puzzling to Western readers, but his "gentle" upbringing renders him helpless against brute force and raw emotions. Ojaknyŏ, a woman of boundless courage and tenacity when it comes to serving and protecting the man she loves but who is at the same time totally selfless in her relationship with him, embodies to Korean men "the eternally feminine." It is worth noting that she comes from the class one rung down the social ladder, and not from the *yangban* class for whom dignity was supposedly more important than life itself.

The Descendants of Cain exhibits many, though by no means all, of Hwang Sun-wŏn's strengths as a writer. The political frenzy and the dark apprehensions it creates are related in simple, spare prose. The emotional tension in Hun and Ojaknyŏ are palpable. Devoid of hyperbole, the novel demonstrates the nobility, cunning, and cruelty latent in the human character, which are brought out by unexpected historical developments. It is a portrait of a society in violent transition. Almost everyone is transformed, including Hun, who surprises himself at the end by deciding to flee with a married woman, something unthinkable under the dictates of conventional morality.

Hwang Sun-wŏn has also written more than one hundred short stories, covering a wide range of subjects and moods, all delicate yet forceful, capturing the personalities, aspirations, and emotions of his characters. Hwang's longer works written in his later years are more ambitious, attempting to examine social and existential life in the context of history and institutions. *The Sun and the Moon* (Ilwŏl, 1964) probes the essential isolation of all human beings by examining the inner conflicts of a rich young man who discovers that his family is descended from a line of butchers, despised social outcasts in traditional Korean society. The young man finally realizes that recovery from existential alienation can begin only with acceptance of who he is.

The Moving Castle (Umjiginŭn Sŏng, 1973) explores the "nomadic" mentality of the Korean people, the clash of Western and traditional cultures, and the possibility of human salvation. Analyses of superstitious beliefs, the problems of urban poverty, religious and nonreligious redemption, and many romantic and not-so-romantic conflicts are woven into the actions and consciousness of the three main characters. The title suggests the adaptability and the instability of the Korean culture and way of life. Hwang's seventh novel, *The Dice of Gods* (Shindŭrŭi Chusawi, 1982) examines the effect of industrialization on the lives and thinking of people in a small town.

Though prevented by his artistic rigor from being prolific, Hwang produced seven novels and five collections of short stories during his nearly five-decade-long writing career. Living through many national crises and tragedies that put his integrity as an artist to severe tests, he tenaciously adhered to his own artistic vision, never giving in to political pressure or commercialism. The Korean public, therefore, reveres him as a consummate artist and a man of true dedication and integrity. His steely asceticism and sagacity as a storyteller seem to make him readily accessible to Western readers as well in spite of his very Korean subject matter and sensibility, and he is currently the most translated Korean author.

Characteristically, Hwang refuses to discuss the "meaning" of his works. In an essay reflecting on his fifty years as a writer, he wrote, "I make it a point never to discuss my works once they are printed. The reason is simple. My works must have lives independent of me. I cannot interfere with the readers' spontaneous appreciation." For the benefit of his Western readers, however, he went so far as to explain to the translators the geography of the novel's setting and some of the dialect and regional vocabularies used. For his assistance and permission to translate the work the translators are deeply grateful. We are also grateful to the Korean Ministry of Culture and Sports for awarding us a translation grant which enabled us to realize our dream of translating this timeless classic. We are also truly beholden to the UNESCO office in Paris, which gave this work its seal of approval, and to the Korean UNESCO commission for its recommendation. Finally, heartfelt thanks go to Mr. Doug Merwin, our present editor, who approved this translation for publication, and Ms. Angela Piliouras who expedited the copyediting and the printing process.

Suh Ji-moon and Julie Pickering
March 1997

The
Descendants
of Cain

1

An icy wind shook the stars that night. It was mid-March, but in the northwest the night air was still biting cold.

A man approached the village along the hilly path that ran past the tavern. It was Pak Hun.

He stumbled along, as if quite drunk. The previous evening, the night school where he had found some satisfaction teaching for the past four months had been shut down by a man from party headquarters. There had been no warning at all. Hun had gone to school at the usual hour, only to find a young man he had never seen before standing at the lectern. It may have been the feeling of emptiness caused by that loss that made him drink so heavily tonight.

To the right of the path was a sloping expanse of newly cleared land, to the left a pine forest. In summer the narrow path was almost entirely overrun with mugwort and wild strawberry vines.

The wind lashed the pines, and the forest moaned like a heavy sea. Hun lifted his head to take the wind full in his face. Though drunk, he smelled pine sap in the icy gust, a sure sign of spring's arrival. He inhaled deeply.

Dark silhouettes of trees began to appear on the slope which rose gently to his right. The trees were part of an orchard belonging to his uncle. Neglected for years, most were blighted and useless now. Hun turned to look at them. They'll blossom again this year, he thought, but the meager fruit will fall and rot before it ripens.

The dark shadows of the orchard spread gradually wider. A fence of acacia saplings, planted around the fruit trees years before, had, for lack of trimming, grown quite large. At the far end of the acacias stood a faint white shadow. It was Ojaknyŏ. She was waiting for him.

Hun recalled the tavern mistress's ribbing earlier that evening. Shouldn't you be getting home, she quipped, if only for poor Ojaknyŏ's sake? Think of her waiting there, craning her neck to catch sight of you. He had simply ignored the remark.

That the villagers talked was no surprise. He and Ojaknyŏ had been living under the same roof for three years, ever since he returned to the village. And it was true: for some time he had found a certain solace in knowing that Ojaknyŏ would be waiting at that same spot every night.

He felt it even now, but realized that his life with her would soon be over. That prospect made him want to play one last practical joke on her. I'll stop here, he thought, and make her come to me.

He stopped short, but the figure at the end of the acacias did not move. Only the wind lashing through the pines grew louder. As one gust raced into the distance, another followed, launching a new assault on the pines. Listening to the wind, Hun suddenly felt that his joke was silly, and he decided to start walking again.

Just then, the figure at the end of the acacias came forward. Hun thought she was running to him, but her pale form cut in front of him and darted into the pine forest. She moved with surprising speed.

Hun snapped to attention. Another shadow seemed to be running ahead of Ojaknyŏ through the pines. His instinct told him it was a man. A shiver ran down his spine, and before he knew it, he was running through the woods after them.

Where did all these jagged stones come from? Hun thought, and the woods are so thick. He stumbled and nearly fell several times, scratching his face and neck on the stiff branches. Still, he ran all out, frantically thrashing the darkness to push the branches aside. The two shadows raced ahead, darting through the woods like wild animals accustomed to the rough terrain.

In the end, Hun lost sight of them. He stopped and listened, but heard nothing, not the slightest trace of human life, only the wind roaring like the sea.

Despite the darkness, he sensed that he was near the old tomb, worn almost flat by the years. To one side of the tomb stood the Mountain Spirit Tree, its dark silhouette looming tall and imposing above the other pines. He flopped down beside the tomb. It was in the middle of a clearing where he went to sun himself from late autumn to early spring.

His throat burned from the short run, and he was sweating. The cuts on his face, neck and hands stung. Weariness flooded through him and he stretched out on the ground. The stars swirled overhead. He closed his eyes. Who could it be? he wondered. Who was Ojaknyŏ chasing? His sweat cooled, and the cold seeping up from the ground sent shivers through his body. The shivers seemed to grow worse as he pondered the identity of the mysterious figure.

One thing was certain—it was a man. And this man was following him or hiding somewhere perhaps, spying on him.

The vague misgivings he had been experiencing now that the so-called land reform was imminent had taken on a certain tangibility in the past few days. They came over him now with new force. The night school had been closed the night before. Who knows what would happen to him next?

As a new wave of shivers passed through his body, he realized he was completely sober.

At any rate, it's time to head home, Hun thought. Stay here much longer and I'm sure to catch a cold. He found it difficult, however, to lift himself from the ground.

The wind subsided for a moment. The silence was palpable and Hun felt isolated, as if floating in a small space all his own. It was eerie. He sensed that someone was hiding somewhere outside that space, watching him. He opened his eyes and sat up with a start.

"We'd better be getting home now," said Ojaknyŏ. She was standing beside him.

Hun rose silently and led the way down the hill. The road home was dark but Hun knew every inch of it, as he had walked it almost every day for the past three years. But for some reason he kept stumbling. He tripped in the brush several times. It wasn't because of the alcohol now, though. It was the thought of that other shadow.

Ojaknyŏ overtook him and acted as a guide, gauging his pace and walking exactly two paces ahead of him.

"Who was that, Ojaknyŏ?"

There was no answer.

"You didn't catch him?"

"No."

"So?"

Again no answer.

"Was it a stranger?"

"No."

"Then who?"

"Sir," said Ojaknyŏ after a moment's silence. Then after another pause, she asked almost pleadingly, "Do you mind if I tell you tomorrow?"

Ojaknyŏ had never evaded his questions before. Something must be seriously wrong. This made Hun all the more anxious to learn the man's identity. And he knew if he pressed her she would tell him. But he didn't. It wouldn't be right to force her to say something she didn't want to say. Now all he wanted to do was go home and lie down.

As they emerged from the woods, the houses of Sunny Hollow came into sight. Lying in an arc with their backs to the path, the houses looked like mounds of straw in the darkness. The largest one, in the middle of the arc, was Hun's.

After taking a dinner tray to Hun, Ojaknyŏ stepped quietly outside. She had to go see her parents. It was time to have it out with them, whatever the cost. How could Samdŭk, her own younger brother, do such a thing? Spying! And on Mr. Pak of all people!

Her parents' tin-roofed house stood about fifty yards from Hun's. She hesitated for an instant as she entered the yard. Her dog Spotty scampered up and rubbed against her legs. Her heart pounded. Then she calmed herself and grasped the door handle.

Her mother was alone. She sat sewing beside the oil lamp. At the sound of the door, she looked up in surprise.

"Oh, is that you?"

"Where'd everyone go?"

"They went out after dinner."

There was a hint of uneasiness and fear in her mother's voice. It seemed to have grown more pronounced lately.

As a girl, Ojaknyŏ's mother was known for her gay laughter. She'd laugh at the slightest provocation. Even after her marriage, with no parents-in-law to constrain her, she would often chat and laugh merrily with the other young women in the village. It wasn't long, however, before all trace of that laughter disappeared from her round, girlish face. It was not because they were poor.

Perhaps it was the dark shadow of her husband, stubborn and unyielding as a stone, that had changed her. Not that he abused her or gave her a hard time. It was as if he were a huge rock that withered the plants in its shade. Crushed by that rock of a husband, Ojaknyŏ's mother lost her smile and a certain shadow took its place. Lately it had become more pronounced. She jumped with fright at the slightest thing.

"Does Samdŭk stay out late every night?"

"Pretty much."

In fact, her son did not stay out late every night, but she exaggerated her anxiety to gain her daughter's sympathy. "I wish they'd stay home at night," she said, as if to herself.

"Why is Father acting this way?"

"I have no idea."

"Why don't you talk to him?"

Her mother turned her frightened eyes on her.

"How can Father act that way to Mr. Pak? He should think of the past. How can he act like that, just because there's going to be land reform? Can't you say something to him, for once in your life?"

Tosŏp, Ojaknyŏ's father, had been Hun's family estate agent for close to thirty years. His life was as comfortable as any landowner's. But now, with the talk of land reform, he had changed completely. That upset Ojaknyŏ.

Her mother's eyes grew even more frightened at her daughter's words. How could she talk like that about her father, whom nobody ever dared to cross? If he found out, there'd be hell to pay.

"And Samdŭk . . . "

"Shhh . . . " Her mother's hand trembled ever so slightly,

then her sewing dropped to the floor. She grabbed her daughter's arm and whispered, "It's your father."

Ojaknyŏ winced and listened. But she heard nothing.

"It's him!" her mother whispered again.

After decades of marriage, the woman recognized her husband's footsteps when no one else could.

A moment later Ojaknyŏ heard someone enter the yard. She jumped up, though she had not meant to avoid her father. As she reached for the door handle she remembered something and turned. "When Samdŭk gets back, tell him to come over to make the fence tomorrow."

But her mother simply bent over her sewing. It was a way of hiding from her husband the anxiety and fear written on her face.

Ojaknyŏ brushed past her father on the stone stoop. Head bent low, she hurried toward the gate. Suddenly she regretted what she had said to her mother. What if Mother does say something to Father? Then she'd be in trouble.

But the next moment, Ojaknyŏ felt a steely resolution rising within her. It was stronger than anything she had felt before. She had to do something. She couldn't put it off forever. Father's wrong, very wrong. He shouldn't treat Mr. Pak like that. And why is Samdŭk acting so strangely?

"Hey girl," her father's gruff voice called out.

Ojaknyŏ stopped dead, as if someone had grabbed her by the nape of her neck.

"Your husband's back."

This time she felt as if she had received a blow on the head. She stood there for a moment, like one not comprehending what she'd heard. Then she rushed away, as if fleeing what she'd heard. She walked as fast as she could.

A whirlwind blew in her ears. "Your husband's back, your husband's back," it sang.

Her head swam. Her legs shook. She felt as if she did not have the strength to hold this body of hers up.

When she reached Hun's house, she grasped the gatepost and leaned against it. Looking up, she saw the light was out in Hun's room.

She collected her thoughts. What am I doing? I left the dinner tray in Mr. Pak's room. I must clear the dishes at once. She had no other thought now.

As she stepped into the yard, her legs were steady, as if something in that house was infusing her with new strength.

Hun hardly touched his dinner before going to bed. Weariness spread through his body and he fell into a troubled dream-ridden sleep.

He was standing in front of the primary school, a long, single-storied building where they held the night school. A light was burning at the center of the building in the classroom they used.

Hun was sick that evening but he had dragged himself out of bed to teach his class. The solitary light in the otherwise dead building made the night school seem alive. He was glad that he had come.

He stepped into the hallway. The night school was held in the first classroom to the right of the entrance.

Class was in session.

He passed the door near the teacher's lectern and went to the back door. He was going to wait in the back of the room for class to finish. He slid open the door as softly as he could. A stranger was addressing the class from the lectern. He was a young man of small stature, wearing a coat made of dog's fur. He spoke with a strong Hamgyŏngdo accent.

Hŭngsu, one of the volunteer teachers, sat on a chair

beside the lectern, his legs crossed as usual. And as usual Ojaknyŏ was sitting by the oil lamp, gazing intently toward the lectern.

Before Hun could step into the room, a young man seated in the back row rose and came over to him. It was Myŏnggu, another volunteer teacher. He pushed Hun into the corridor and whispered. "He's from party headquarters." Hun caught only a snatch of what the young man was saying. "The most important question in education is 'Who's teaching who.' In other words, the class backgrounds of the instructor and the pupils."

Hun went outside, but somehow he could still see what was going on in the schoolroom. He searched for Ojaknyŏ. She wasn't in her spot by the lamp. He found her sitting forlornly in a dark corner. The light in her eyes was gone.

Ojaknyŏ was normally simple and modest, but a peculiar light burned in her eyes when she sat by the lamp at the night school. A remarkable intelligence emanated from her eyes, and she learned more quickly than the rest. Tonight, however, her eyes were dull, and she sat alone in that dark corner.

Suddenly, she stood up. She stepped from the shadows to approach the lamp and blew it out, as if to say its light too was no longer needed.

Myŏnggu drew near. "This is our last class," he whispered. Pulch'ul began shoving the chairs against the wall. He was the young man who lit the stove each night and tidied up after class. Tonight, he was tidying the room as if this were the last class.

Hyŏk, Hun's cousin, urged him to go home.

Hun stood in the darkness, feeling shivers and aches running down his spine.

He was outside again, waiting for Ojaknyŏ by the entrance. But she did not appear. I'll wait for her forever, he thought, but in fact it wasn't Hun who was waiting; it was Ojaknyŏ. And she was waiting not at the entrance to the school but at the corner of the orchard on the path home. She was waiting for him with a lamp in her hand.

Hun felt like playing a practical joke on her. He hid behind a pine tree, but she found him in no time. He began running through the woods, and she ran after him. Earlier that evening Hun had run after her, but in the dream she chased him.

There's no need to run from her, he thought, but he kept running. He stumbled over rocks and scratched his face, neck and hands on branches.

I hope she catches me, he thought, and then she did.

She began kissing the cuts on his face. She kissed the wounds on his neck. She even kissed the scratches on the back of his hands and arms.

Next she began to lick him with her tongue. She licked his forehead, his shoulders, then his chest. His skin tingled with embarrassment.

Yet he didn't push her away. Instead, he gave himself up to her entirely, feeling exquisitely content.

Then he realized that her lamp was burning with a dazzling brightness. Maybe it was because of her glowing eyes. To be thus exposed he felt embarrassed, but, at the same time, happy.

Suddenly, he worried that someone might see them like this. He asked her to put out the lamp, but she paid him no heed.

He blew at the flame. It wouldn't go out. He blew again and again. It kept burning. He tried harder and harder—and then he woke up.

Ojaknyŏ was looking at him. The lamp burned brightly. He realized that she had applied mercurochrome to his scratches and was wiping the sweat from his body.

"You seem awfully sick. You were sweating and kept talking in your sleep." She looked worried.

"I'm all right," he said. It wasn't the first time he'd had those symptoms.

"I came in to clear the dishes and saw you were bleeding," she said, as if to apologize for entering his room at night. "You have cuts all over, and your skin feels clammy. Lately you haven't looked well." She sounded as if she held herself responsible for his illness.

"I'm all right," he said, then closed his eyes, fearful that he might have betrayed his feelings.

"Could you put out the lamp?" he asked, but then he recalled saying the same thing in his dream.

"No," he said, "Leave it on."

His eyes seemed even more hollow tonight. His damp forehead looked especially broad under the bright lamp. He was only twenty-nine but looked years older.

After a while his pointed jaw moved ever so slightly. He moistened his parched lips with the tip of his tongue. Then he turned, as if to avoid the lamplight.

A night cuckoo sang in the darkness. The wind swept through the pines, carrying off the cuckoo's song, then returned.

Hun remembered a scene from his childhood. He had awakened from a bad dream in the middle of the night and heard the call of a night cuckoo ringing through the darkness. It reminded him of the legend of Maiden Rock. He had burrowed into his mother's bosom, and his fear had melted in the warm coziness.

He tried to revive the exquisite coziness he had felt in his mother's arms, but instead recalled the contentment he had experienced in his dream when he gave himself up to Ojaknyŏ's caresses. He pulled the covers over his head.

Ojaknyŏ listened to the cuckoo. She had forgotten that it was time to return to her own room. And as she listened, her eyes burned with a new light, the light of a dream.

2

Hun heard the door slide open. He could tell someone had entered the room.

"Are you sick?"

It was his cousin Hyŏk.

Hun wasn't sleeping, but strangely he didn't feel quite awake, either.

"Why, what happened to your face?" Hyŏk asked, laying his hand on Hun's forehead.

Hun opened his eyes. The room was so bright it made him blink. Sunlight was pouring through the south window. Outside, the wind seemed to have subsided.

"You don't have a temperature. What happened? Did you fall down?"

"No." Hun shut his eyes again.

Hyŏk drew closer and whispered in his ear. "Did you hear?" He paused. "Kwŏn's dead."

Suddenly Hun felt wide awake.

"He died last night, got stabbed with a sickle." Hyŏk's face was directly above Hun's. It was flushed with excitement.

"His wife said she woke up in the night and felt something damp. At first she thought the baby had wet the bed, but it felt too sticky for that. When she sat up, she found a sickle stuck in Kwŏn's chest. She'd heard something in her sleep, like the door opening and shutting, but she just assumed it was her husband going to the outhouse. It must have been the murderer."

For a farmer, Kwŏn was sickly. It was thanks to his dire poverty that he had been appointed chairman of the local peasant committee not long ago.

"It looks like the swords have finally been drawn."

Hun agreed. He felt a hot surge in his chest. He hadn't felt that way in a long time. With the communists tightening their noose around former landlords and intellectuals, it was no wonder someone had struck back.

Still, Hun recalled the flock of half-starved children in Kwŏn's family. They all had such big, dark eyes.

The eldest had died of malnutrition the year before liberation. Kwŏn wasn't home at the time. He had been conscripted into service on an irrigation project in Anju. His wife was at the market in Sunan, selling steamed corn as usual. When she returned that evening, flies were swarming over the child's sunken eyes and gaping mouth. She had been dead for several hours, but the younger children didn't know it. They thought their sister had been sleeping all day.

"We don't know who did it yet, but it's pretty obvious which side they were on, don't you think?"

Hun looked up at his cousin's plump face. The instant he heard of Kwŏn's murder he knew which side did it. And he felt sure they were in for more bloodshed. But knowing that Kwŏn had only been an innocent instrument of the party, he could not help feeling sorry for the dead farmer.

"Cousin, you look awfully sick. You'd better take some medicine."

"No, I'm all right."

"Well, take care of yourself. I have to go now. Who would have dared do such a thing?"

Hyŏk stood up. He was still excited by the news. A shaft of sunlight struck his broad chest and fell to the floor.

Hun closed his eyes to shut out the light. His cousin's brisk steps faded beyond the gate. Suddenly, Hun felt he had something to tell his cousin. Then he felt rising in his heart a kind of anger directed at no one in particular, an anger bordering on a certain sorrow.

Tosŏp, Ojaknyŏ's father, was sitting in the night-duty room at the local people's committee office, across from a party operative sent from military headquarters, the young man in the dog-fur coat.

"Comrade, I won't hold your past against you if you serve the people faithfully from now on."

"I'll do anything you say, sir. Just tell me what you want me to do."

His two-and-a-half decades as estate agent on Hun's family land were a liability now.

"First of all, you must sever your ties with that landlord."

"I already have, completely."

"You'll have to prove that by your actions."

"I'll do anything you tell me, sir."

"Don't call me sir. Call me comrade." The young man lowered his voice. "Well, comrade . . . Did you notice anything unusual at Pak's house last night?"

Tosŏp hesitated, trying to figure out what would qualify as "unusual."

"I mean, did you see anyone going in or out of the house?" the young man explained.

Tosŏp tilted his shaven head. "The light in his room was burning late into the night."

"Has anybody been coming to the house regularly?"

"Well, his cousin Hyŏk, and that young man named Myŏnggu."

"Did this Myŏnggu fellow come to see him last night?"

"I saw the two of them talking on the hill behind the village yesterday afternoon."

"What about Pulch'ul?"

"He rarely comes."

The young man nodded. "Now, comrade, we'd like you to succeed our late lamented comrade who died at the hands of the bourgeois terrorists last night. Our work must continue without interruption. As the chairman of the peasant committee, you must make a clean break from your old landlord, and fight ruthlessly for the revolution. That's the only way you can atone for your past."

Tosŏp felt immensely relieved. When he heard that he had been ordered to appear before the local people's committee, he thought he was finished.

As he walked home, a smirk played at the corners of his mouth, which was shaved as smooth as his head.

Good thing I already cut my ties with that old landlord, he thought. I must take care not to have anything to do with him in the future, he told himself.

And then he had another thought. Kwŏn had been murdered because he was a weakling. I may be old but no one'd dare lay a finger on me. Just let 'em try, he thought. They'll see. Tosŏp coughed up a wad of phlegm and spat it to the side of the road.

An errand boy from the police station came to call Hun to the station. Ojaknyŏ offered to go and find out what they wanted, but Hun told her that was unnecessary and got out of bed. He still felt slightly dizzy.

The police station was just a few doors away from the people's committee headquarters, on the main road leading to Sunan. Hun found three men waiting for him there. A uniformed policeman sat behind a desk; the young man in the dog-fur coat sat at a conference table to one side, and Hŭngsu sat in a chair against the opposite wall. The three men thus formed a triangle facing Hun.

"Have a seat. I'm sorry to make you come all the way down here," the policeman began politely. "We have a few questions to ask you. When did you first open the night school?"

"In late October last year."

"And who helped you start it?"

"Besides myself there was my cousin, a young man called Myŏnggu, and Mr. Pyŏn over there."

Pyŏn Hŭngsu's eyes were fixed on the policeman. Not once did he look in Hun's direction. He had been appointed chairman of the local Democratic Youth Committee the day before.

"What subjects did you teach?"

"Korean language and history."

"Do you regard Tan'gun* as an actual historical figure?"

"Well, the history of any nation begins with a mythical or legendary period."

"What I want to know is . . . " the policeman interrupted, then glanced at the young man in the dog-fur coat as if he needed prompting. The young man simply stared into space. The policeman dropped his eyes to a piece of paper on the desk in front of him.

"You must tell us whether you portrayed Tan'gun as a historical figure in your lectures or not."

---

*Tan'gun is the legendary founder of ancient Korea. His father is Hwanung, the heavenly emperor's son who came down to earth to teach and befriend men, and his mother is the female bear who successfully transformed herself into a woman by withstanding the one hundred days' trial in a dark cave. He allegedly founded the original Chosŏn Dynasty in 2333 B.C.

"During the tribal period there may have been a prominent leader, and he may have been called Tan'gun, but it's simply a myth, a legend . . ."

"That's enough! It's clear you treated Tan'gun as a real person," the young man interjected, his eyes still staring in front of him.

Hun wanted to explain further, but decided against it. The debate would go on forever. Then a thought occurred to him: the young man in the dog-fur coat looked familiar.

The policeman continued, glancing at the notes on his desk. "What did your cousin teach?"

"Mathematics."

"And this Myŏnggu fellow?"

"He taught agriculture, as did Mr. Pyŏn here."

"Why didn't Myŏnggu come to school last night?"

"I don't know."

"You didn't come because you were ill, but what about Myŏnggu? Was there some reason why he didn't attend?"

"Not as far as I know. Perhaps he wanted to study more before he taught others."

"Where's Myŏnggu now?"

"He lives in Chestnut Hollow."

"I know. I'm asking where he went last night."

"Last night?"

"Yes, he disappeared last night. You must know where he's gone."

"No, I don't."

"Didn't he say anything to you?"

"Say what?"

"That's what we'd like to know," the young man cut in.

"I haven't heard anything."

"When did you last see Myŏnggu?" the policeman resumed, checking the notes again.

"Yesterday."

"What did you talk about?"

"Nothing much. I was sitting on the hill, and he came up and sat next to me. We just sat there for a while, then he stood up and said I didn't look well and told me to take better care of myself."

The young man leaned forward as if to say something, then exhaled a puff of cigarette smoke instead.

The police officer looked at the paper again. "What did you do last night?"

"I went to the tavern for a drink."

"The one run by Pulch'ul's mother? Did you see Pulch'ul there?"

"No, I didn't."

The policeman glanced at the young man again, then dropped his eyes to the paper.

"Your light was burning late into the night, wasn't it?"

"I wasn't feeling well."

The young man snuffed out his cigarette against the side of the table. "You drank quite a bit last night, didn't you?"

"Yes."

"Even though you were sick?"

"I wasn't really sick. I suffer from insomnia when the season changes. Alcohol helps me sleep."

"How did you get those cuts on your face?"

"I guess I drank too much last night."

"Is this yours?" The young man placed a book on the table.

"Yes."

It was a volume from a series on world philosophy. The young man opened the book to an earmarked page.

"I see you have underlined phrases like 'dictatorship of the proletariat' and 'terrorism.' Why?"

"Actually, Myŏnggu did that. He used to underline words and passages he didn't understand and ask me what they meant. I suppose they were a bit difficult for him since he only had two years at the agricultural high school."

"All right. Now, let's get straight to the point. Yesterday, the chairman of the peasant committee was murdered by terrorists. Myŏnggu and Pulch'ul did it. We must find them. That's why we called you down here."

"As I told you, I don't know where they are."

"Forget Pulch'ul. Just tell us where Myŏnggu is."

"I really don't know."

"I'm not begging you to tell us. I'm ordering you. It's your duty to obey me!" The young man jumped from his chair. "Don't think you can fool me. Your night school was a cover for a reactionary plot. A ploy to seduce innocent peasants! Telling them all sorts of flagrant lies, like the one that Tan'gun founded our country. We can see right through you and all the other reactionaries. You wrap history in an aura of myth to disguise the true process of historical development. You're not going to get away with it this time, though. History belongs to the proletariat, no matter what tricks you play. Look at Soviet Russia, the fatherland of the proletariat. Do you think you can keep the peasants as your slaves? Never! The peasants and laborers are launching a desperate battle against you capitalists and landowners. We're driven by a violent hatred, and we will emerge victorious! There is no doubt about it. We have the support of the great benefactor and liberator of the downtrodden, Stalin." Sparks flew from the young man's eyes as he glared at Hun.

"By closing your night school we put an end to your intrigue, but you reactionaries devised a new conspiracy—the murder of the chairman of the peasant committee. I know you've been plotting this for a long time. First, you bought off Pulch'ul. It was easy enough to lure that gambling addict with money. You made him your tool and sent him to the peasant committee chairman's house every night, pretending he was making social calls. You were waiting for the right moment, and then you had him murder the peasants' leader. Pulch'ul committed the murder. The murder weapon is proof enough. Sickles aren't like knives. They're hard to handle if you haven't used one before. Pulch'ul committed the murder, but he couldn't have planned it. Someone else was the mastermind. Kwŏn was stabbed right in the heart. And it was pitch dark at the time. That was no coincidence as far as I'm concerned. Clearly someone put a lot of time into training Pulch'ul. Myŏnggu is one of the conspirators. He's the son of a reactionary owner-cultivator and landlord. I don't think he planned this on his own, though. Someone else was clearly pulling the strings.

"You say you know nothing. But we're going to get to the bottom of this! You can't hide anything from us. We'll unearth your secrets, no matter how deep they're buried. It's just like your accent. You speak the Seoul dialect because you went to high school and college there, but your P'yŏngando accent gives you away, just as I can't get rid of my Hamgyŏngdo accent. Our true colors always come through in the end.

"You won't be forgiven when we uncover your involvement. We will avenge our comrade's murder a thousand times over, no, ten thousand times over. We could lock you up right now if we wanted. We have enough evidence. We won't, though. We don't arrest and imprison people the way the Japanese imperialists did. But remember this: From now on, you're not allowed to step beyond a mile radius of this village without our permission!"

The young man sat down.

Hun rose from his seat. His mind was a blank, except for the realization that it was this young man who had come to the night school and said, *The most important question in education is "Who's teaching who?" In other words, the class backgrounds of the instructor and the pupils.*

Hun clung to this recollection, for lack of a better way of holding himself together.

Hŭngsu remained seated, stiff and erect, in the chair by the wall, his eyes fixed on the policeman.

The sound of yelling jerked Hun to his senses. He had reached the Mountain Spirit Tree, though he didn't remember crossing the ridge.

The yells came from Tosŏp's front yard. Hun couldn't make out the words, but he recognized Tosŏp's angry voice.

Hun flung himself to the ground.

Tosŏp was jerking Ojaknyŏ about by the hair. "Why don't you drop dead, you miserable whore?" he bellowed.

Her hands clasped around her head, Ojaknyŏ stumbled after her father. A deadly pallor had spread over her face and her expression was blank, as if she were too stunned to feel anything.

Her mother, who had been standing to the side trembling helplessly, at last managed to summon up the courage to draw closer and reach for her husband's hand. "Please let her go and try to talk it out," she pleaded.

"You keep out of this," Tosŏp snarled and sent her tumbling with a shove of his elbow. "This whore's trying to tell her father what to do! Death would be too good for her!"

Hun had seen this frightening side of Tosŏp once before, back when he was in middle school.

He had come to spend his winter vacation at his grand-parents'. There was a bean threshing in Tosŏp's yard that day. Tosŏp's family lived just a few houses from Hun's grandparents at the time.

Hun was standing to the side watching the threshing when a middle-aged farmer appeared. The man's beard was stained yellow with nicotine. Hun had never seen him before.

The farmer stood in one corner, as if he had no special reason for being there. Tosŏp didn't seem to notice his presence. He went on with his threshing, circling the yard quite naturally, until he reached the man. Then he yelled, "No!"

The man quietly reached in the pocket of his worn cotton vest and took out a pipe. Then he took out his flint stones and began talking to Tosŏp in a low voice. Hun could not make out what he was saying over the sound of the threshing.

"I said, No," shouted Tosŏp as he thrust his thresher into the man's shoulder, and sent him crashing to the ground. His lips curving into a bitter smile, the man tried to stand but Tosŏp's thresher knocked him down again. The stranger tried to get up once more. The thresher fell on him again. Blood poured from his nose and lips and from behind his ear.

Hun rushed over to Tosŏp and grabbed the handle of his thresher, but he was no match for the older man. The thresher bore down on the stranger with relentless regularity.

Tosŏp's face remained completely expressionless through-out the beating. His head was shaven razor-smooth as al-ways, a cotton towel twisted tightly around it, and his face too was clean-shaven. Black upturned eyebrows were the only hairs on his square face. And his solid jaw was thrust stubbornly forward. His face was as expressionless as when he threshed bean stalks.

Hun trembled, helpless and bewildered. Someone ran up and tried to help the man to his feet. It was Ojaknyŏ. The thresher crashed down on her back. She staggered and almost fell. If the thresher had hit her once more, she would surely have collapsed.

Before he knew what he was doing, Hun ran to her and shielded her, his arms stretched wide. She turned to him, then looked away. Her eyes were round and large, as always. When he looked into those eyes, he forgot that the thresher might come down on him next.

It didn't, though. Even Tosŏp couldn't beat his master's son. Ojaknyŏ helped the stranger to his feet. Hun learned later that it was for no great matter that the stranger was treated so harshly. The farmer with the yellowed beard was a tenant on Hun's father's land, like nearly everyone else in the area. A few days earlier he had asked Tosŏp to let him split the harvest in the coming year instead of paying a fixed rent. Tosŏp had refused, but the man had returned that day to plead with him once more, only to be flailed for his effort. Hun's father had already entrusted the management of all his land to Tosŏp by that time.

Hun had feared Tosŏp after the thresher incident. But, when Hun's father passed away, Tosŏp grieved more bitterly than anyone, even Hun himself. Perhaps it was because the one person who had truly appreciated him was gone. Hun had never seen a middle-aged man cry with such wrenching sorrow. It made him feel that Tosŏp was not a cold blooded man after all, and he decided to entrust everything to Tosŏp, as his father had done before him.

After his father's death, Hun decided to close the house in Pyongyang and return to the country, hoping thereby to avoid conflicts with the Japanese, whose demands were growing harsher as the end of the war drew near. It was two years before liberation.

He already had a site for his new house. It was in Sunny Hollow, near the crossroads. His father had chosen the site. If his father had not died so suddenly from a heart attack, the house would have been built much sooner. Tosŏp took care of everything, from drawing the ground plan to laying the foundation and supervising the builders. The work began in late fall, which meant a great rush. Moreover, building materials were scarce because of the war.

So they ended up building a very modest house. The central wing consisted of a medium-sized main room, a small kitchen and small side room. The outer wing was simply a shed connected to the main gate. They could only afford to spread one layer of mud on the outer walls and had to abandon their original plan for a stone wall in favor of a millet stalk fence. They managed to get tiles for the roof, but the lumber was of poor quality. All in all, the house was a rather shabby affair. There was, however, a well in the backyard. They had it dug first to provide water to make the mud for the walls.

When the house was ready, Hun needed someone to cook and clean for him. Tosŏp suggested Ojaknyŏ, who had returned home to escape her abusive husband.

The first thing that came to his mind at the mention of Ojaknyŏ was her glowing eyes. Hun had met several women while studying in Seoul and later when he returned to Pyongyang, but each time the relationship was about to develop into something serious, he recalled Ojaknyŏ's eyes and nothing would come of it. He never met any woman whose eyes could equal hers. Once, at his parents' insistence, he had almost gotten engaged. She was a fine woman in every way, but he had balked at marrying her. I don't like her eyes, he had said.

After returning to his village, Hun saw Ojaknyŏ around the neighborhood from time to time, though only from behind for she seemed to make a point of avoiding him. Her slender figure had ripened into that of a mature woman.

This was the Ojaknyŏ who came to keep house for Hun. At first, she stayed with her parents and took care of the household work during the day, but after Hun was bedridden by a bad cold, she moved into the side room.

Her eyes hadn't changed. She rarely looked at him straight on, though. Her face had retained its soft, clear complexion despite the sun, but each time she encountered him she turned away shyly.

An air of sorrow seemed to envelop her entire being. The once cheerful girl had changed. Hun attributed this change to her failed marriage. Meeting her again after more than a decade, he felt a certain melancholy.

The countryside offered no refuge from the war. On the contrary, the pressure was even more intense there. He could see it with his naked eye, feel it with his skin, but somehow, he felt he could bear it, if only Ojaknyŏ would remain by his side.

The defeat of Japan brought liberation. Hun had two more coats of mud stucco applied to the outer walls. He had the well cleaned, and stones collected for a wall to replace the makeshift millet stalk fence. Tosŏp supervised everything.

Ojaknyŏ's attitude also changed with time. She no longer kept her eyes lowered in his presence. She began waiting for him when he went out, and in the evenings would even go to meet him at the corner of the orchard. Hun's heart warmed at the thought of her waiting for him.

They collected enough stones for a low wall, but they now

lay neglected in a pile. The lattices on the millet stalk fence had to be replaced, if nothing else, but Tosŏp didn't bother to do anything about it. There had already been talk of read-justing the crop share to make the split more favorable to the tenants.

Lately, Tosŏp seemed to be avoiding Hun, to say nothing of his neglect of Hun's fence. When he ran into Hun in the street, he averted his face and hurried past him. He started behaving this way when rumors that the landlords' holdings would be confiscated and redistributed to the peasants began circulating among the villagers.

It's all because of the times, Hun thought.

He could still hear Tosŏp yelling in his yard.

"You bitch, stop being his housemaid! Don't you have any pride?"

"You shouldn't act that way to Mr. Pak!" Ojaknyŏ cried in return, reeling left and right as her father shook her by the hair.

"What? You want me to kill you right here and now?"

"What's wrong with leaving a lamp lit in a sick room?"

"Child, you keep your mouth shut!" Ojaknyŏ's mother cried, as she sat crumpled on the ground, trembling in fear of her husband.

"How could you report it to the police?" the daughter persisted.

"I'll kill you!" Tosŏp threw Ojaknyŏ on the ground and stepped on the back of her neck. She gasped, her face in the dirt and all four limbs sprawled out.

"I'm going to kill this whore right here! How dare you go into a man's room at night! You dirty whore! Your husband's still alive. Alive!" He kicked her again.

"Go ahead . . . Kill me! Why don't you . . . put an end to . . . my misery once and for all!" Ojaknyŏ gasped.

Her mother clawed at the ground, moaning, "Help, help!"

Samdŭk, who had been watching all this in silence at some distance, approached his father. In fact, his mother had wanted to ask for his help from the beginning, but she was afraid her son would be beaten as well.

Samdŭk grabbed his father's arm. Tosŏp tried to shake him off, but he could not break Samdŭk's grip. Samdŭk then grasped the hand holding his sister's hair and began loosening the fingers one by one.

"You son of a bitch!" Tosŏp growled as he tightened his grip. But his son forced the fingers open. Tosŏp shot a look of surprise at his son, as if astonished that Samdŭk had grown so strong. The next moment, however, he hollered at his son to get out of the way and reached for his daughter's hair again. Samdŭk jumped between them, and caught his father in his arms.

"Run, sister, quickly! I'll come over to make the fence tomorrow," Samdŭk shouted.

"You, son of a bitch!" Tosŏp swung his fist at his son, but Samdŭk caught his arm. Tosŏp struggled to shove his son away but ended up taking a step backward instead. Next, he tried holding his ground, but was forced further backward.

"How dare you treat your father this way, you miserable brat?"

Samdŭk did not stop until they reached the brushwood gate. Tosŏp snatched the pole from the A-frame carrier but Samdŭk already had a firm grip on the other end. Tosŏp glared at his son. His thick black eyebrows twitched violently. His arm trembled and he let go of the pole.

"I wish you'd drop dead, all of you! You whore, you're not my daughter anymore. Don't you ever call me father again. And you lousy son of a bitch, I'll chop off your hands if you make that bastard's fence for him."

Tosŏp stepped onto the earthen floor between the two main rooms, squatted down, and lit his bamboo pipe. After smoking nearly a full bowl, he seemed to have recovered a measure of calm. It suddenly occurred to him that he was old now and could no longer control his children. But the next minute he thought, those young fools don't see what's happening. They don't realize they'll be in big trouble if they keep kow-towing to their old landlord. I've got to do something to get us through this, he thought. Fresh beads of sweat began forming on his wrinkled brow.

Hun came down from the hill. He passed his house and went to the crossroads. Beside the intersection of the three roads leading to Chin'gol, the town of Sunan, and Karakkol stood a stone monument. It was a marble stele with a pointed top, commemorating Hun's grandfather's munificence as a landlord.

A dozen or so thatched houses lined the roads near the monument. The hut beside the well facing the monument belonged to Ko Subok. Ko was in his seventies and lived alone with his grandson, Tangson. Hun visited the old man from time to time.

Old Ko was weaving a straw sack with his grandson. His hair and beard were immaculately white.

"What happened to your face?" the old man asked, looking up as Hun approached.

"I guess I drank too much last night."

"You have to take better care of yourself. You shouldn't drink too much. You were never very strong. And now there's all this trouble . . . "

"Well, I'll try to be more careful. By the way, is it true that Tosŏp comes from a landowning family?"

"Oh, yes. His family used to live in Yŏngyu. His grandfather owned a lot of land up there. He was a big man in those parts. Tosŏp grew up wanting nothing, till his father squandered the family fortune on some gold mine."

"So that's when they moved here."

"No. I believe they roamed the country for many years. . . . Had a real hard life. It must have been especially hard for young Tosŏp. They say he had a private tutor when he was little."

Hun knew that Tosŏp must have had some learning, as he handled the bookkeeping without any assistance.

"He must have been in his twenties when he came to this village. He met your father soon after, and things have been going fine for him ever since. Got married here, too."

"My father put him in charge of everything."

"Yes. And Tosŏp did a fine job, though at times he was too hard on the tenants. He always said you have to rule them with an iron fist or there'd be no end to their begging and pleading. If a tenant rubbed him the wrong way, he'd make the man's life a hell. Why, I daresay he ended up getting more holiday chickens and rice cakes from the tenants than your father did! From time to time, your father'd tell him not to be so harsh on the tenants, and then he'd gripe how the landlord wouldn't let him do his job. From what I've heard, your father used to say that once you've trusted someone with a job, you have to let him go about it in his own way."

The old man picked up a handful of rice straw and began plucking off the empty kernels.

"Did you hear about Kwŏn?"

"Yes, Tangson found out this morning. It's a pity such a nice fellow had to end up like that! He didn't have any enemies. What's the world coming to? What kind of devil would do such a thing?"

Hun could hardly say Myŏnggu and Pulch'ul were proba-bly responsible for it. It may have been true, but he couldn't bring himself to put his suspicions into words.

"I feel even worse for his family. His wife says they don't have any spare bedclothes, so she has to wash that bloodstained quilt and use it."

The old man turned away, and as he picked up the warp guide, he muttered. "What will become of this world?"

Sliding the guide downward, he spoke again, this time to Hun. "Oh, you know, that . . . guy's back."

"Who do you mean?" Hun asked, not comprehending.

"Ojaknyŏ's husband. Haven't seen him around for a few years, but he passed by here yesterday."

Hun thought he could piece it all together now. The mys-terious figure in the woods last night must have been Ojaknyŏ's husband. No wonder she didn't want to tell me who it was.

Yes, it's time for me to leave the village, Hun thought. Then he heard a voice. *You're not allowed to step beyond a mile radius of this village without our permission!* Well, I guess I'll just have to stay. Somehow, he felt relieved that he had no choice but to remain in the village. At the same time, that feeling of relief frightened him.

Hun stood up and said goodbye to his old neighbor.

He ran into Hyŏk in front of the well.

"Oh, there you are! I've been looking for you," Hyŏk said, then drew closer and whispered in his ear. "Myŏnggu and Pulch'ul did it." Hyŏk paused to study Hun's reaction, then whispered again: "I never dreamed they'd be so brave."

The evening sun accentuated the color in Hyŏk's flushed face.

Hun started up the hill toward home without comment.

Hyŏk thought his cousin was acting rather strangely that day. After taking a few steps, Hun turned to look back, as if he suddenly remembered something he had to tell his cousin, but Hyŏk was already out of earshot. He strode along vigorously, like the young student he was. Hyŏk was enrolled in a technical high school in Seoul. He had come home for summer vacation the previous year and had been prevented from returning to school by the division of the country following liberation.

As he gazed at Hyŏk striding away briskly, Hun once again felt that anger so akin to sorrow.

Ojaknyŏ held her head even lower than usual as she brought in Hun's supper that evening. Her husband's return may have been the cause of the fight with her father that day. Yes, it's time I left the village, Hun thought once again.

He noticed a scratch on her chin as she turned to leave the room.

"Wait . . . You've got quite a cut there."

She paused with her back to him. "It's nothing."

He stood up and moistened some cotton with mercurochrome. "Here," he said.

"It's nothing," she repeated, shaking her head gently. Her hair was combed back in a neat bun as usual.

"It'll only take a second," he insisted.

Only then did she turn to him, shy and submissive. She closed her eyes softly while he applied the medicine. Her eyelids were swollen. She must have been crying.

The color returned to her wan face. It spread from behind her ears, over her cheeks, eyes and nose. When it reached the tip of her nose, her eyelids quivered. Then drops of dew rolled out of her closed eyes and broke as they streaked down her cheeks. Her face trembled, then her shoulders and bosom heaved. Her lower body shook. Her entire body quaked.

She didn't realize it, though. All she knew was that her body felt weightless, as if it were about to float into the air. She simply stood there, giving herself over to Hun's caring hands.

That night, the villagers gathered around a fire in O Manlip's front yard by the crossroads.

"I hear land reform's already been enforced in Kanggye," Kim Pokdong remarked to Carpenter Kang.

"Yes. In Yŏngbyŏn, too, they say," responded Kang, a farmer who had earned the nickname "carpenter" because of his carpentry skills. The villagers called on him whenever they built a new house or repaired an old one, and he often volunteered to make chicken coops or A-frame carriers, or even whittle handles for grindstones.

Kang was also always the first to bring rumors from the outside.

"So, what's this land reform all about?" O Manlip asked, addressing no one in particular. Of course it wasn't as if he hadn't heard of land reform before. In fact, ever since the land reform ordinance was passed on March 5, he had heard countless rumors about how land was going to be distributed to farmers for free. He simply couldn't believe it. Land for free? Nothing's free in this life!

O Manlip was not the only one who felt that way. Everyone there felt the same way. Of course, that didn't mean the prospect didn't appeal to them. Imagine—land of our own! Their hearts jumped at the very thought of it!

But the next moment they felt guilty, as if they were wishing for something they shouldn't. They tapped their pipes on the ground, blew their noses, or cleared their throats to hide their guilty feelings.

"In one village I hear they hitched all the single men and women, the widows and widowers, too," Kang said, glad to come up with a topic that didn't relate to land. "Yes, they gathered all the single folk in one place and made them play this game, kind of like hide-and-seek. You married the first person you caught."

"Wow, that sure leaves a lot to chance," Kim Pokdong commented. "But hey, we have our fair share of single folk. It might be fun to try something like that."

"But what if Yi Kapsŏng gets Granny Bullye?"

Everyone laughed at Manlip's joke. Granny Bullye was a widow well over seventy, and Kapsŏng was just twenty. Kapsŏng, totally unabashed, joked, "I'm going to get T'anshil."

A fresh wave of laughter rose. T'anshil, Manlip's daughter, was a nubile girl of seventeen.

"Damn you!" Manlip muttered, but he joined in the laughter.

They all laughed unnaturally loud and long, as if to hide the confusion that had overcome them lately.

Then suddenly everyone stopped laughing. All eyes turned in one direction. Tosŏp was standing behind them, carrying a bucket of water.

"What are you idiots sitting around gabbing about at a time like this? Kang, you've only made the coffin. What about a grave marker? See if the bier needs repair, too. And why aren't the rest of you at Kwŏn's house?"

Tosŏp threw the bucket of water on the fire. The villagers sprang up, as if he had thrown the water on them.

The dead man's house was teeming with mourners. Many had to sit on the dirt floor between Kwŏn's kitchen and room. They were all impressed to see how important the post of peasant committee chairman was. Hun was about to leave to make room for new arrivals when Kim, the village doctor, called to him from across the room.

"What do you think, Mr. Pak? I believe that the most important things in life should be free."

What is this man trying to say, Hun wondered as he gazed at the doctor's bald head. Dr. Kim had been bald since he first came to the village in his late twenties a decade and a half ago.

"Take air, for example. We can't live without it, and it's free. And water. I hear you have to pay for water in the city, but I imagine it's the cheapest thing you can buy. That's because we all have to have water. But what about food? We can't live without it either, but for some reason, the people who grow food starve, and the people who have nothing to do with growing it have more than they know what to do with.

"Now, why is this? It's because of the greedy landowning class. People who have nothing to do with the land act like they own it! Is that fair? The land should belong to those who till it. That's why I've already donated my small plot of land to the government, to be distributed to farmers."

Dr. Kim mopped the sweat from his brow and glanced to the corner where two young strangers were sitting. They had probably been sent from party headquarters.

Hun recalled reading something similar to what Dr. Kim had said. He figured the doctor had made a point of telling him so people would know he had cooperated with land reform.

Dr. Kim's clinic stood in front of the town office. He had started out in a thatched house, but in just a couple of years he had managed to build himself a tiled-roof house with flying rafters. He was rumored to refuse poor patients. He was also rumored to dabble in usury. With each passing year he bought a few more parcels of land. He had become a sizeable landowner before liberation.

Hun glanced at the coffin as he rose again to leave. It was wrapped in a long piece of white cotton cloth. The local people's committee had provided the cloth, together with half a sack of rice. Hun recalled old Ko saying that the dead man's wife had to wash the bloody quilt because they had no spare bedding. The fine cotton cloth seemed out of place in this house, so white against the soot-covered walls which reeked of damp mud.

Nami, Kwŏn's son, rushed out of the kitchen cupping a lump of cooked rice in his hands. A girl with disheveled hair scrambled after him. Staving off his sister with his shoulder, the boy stuffed the rice into his mouth. Bits of sticky rice clung to his nose, lips and cheeks. His sister snatched his hand and bit it. Nami screamed and jerked back his hand, but he was soon licking his palm again. Hun could not bear to watch any longer.

3

The next morning, Samdŭk came to work on Hun's fence. His father pretended not to notice him leaving. The boy wouldn't listen to him anyway. Tosŏp gazed at his son's broad shoulders. He isn't a child anymore, he thought, but in the next instant, his pride gave way to anger. That boy doesn't understand how the world works. Who knows what'll happen to our family if he keeps this up? Tosŏp fumed but knew he would only lose face if he tried to reason with the boy. He hacked up a gob of phlegm and looked away.

Hun was sitting on the veranda. Why bother fixing the fence now? he thought. In Yŏngbyŏn and Pakch'ŏn, they've already carried out land reform and the landlords are being driven from their homes. There was no telling when his turn would come.

Hun stepped into the courtyard. He thought he would take a walk, if only to the hill behind the village. As he headed out the gate, he heard Ojaknyŏ's quiet voice reprimanding her brother: "Why did you follow Mr. Pak the other day?"

Hun's heart sank and he stopped in his tracks. So it was Samdŭk, not Ojaknyŏ's husband, who had followed him the night before last. But why? That sensation, a feeling heavier than sorrow, which came over him lately as he encountered changes in his old neighbors, descended on him again. Samdŭk made no reply.

"Tell me! Why did you do such a thing?"

Only the rustling of millet stalks answered.

"What's wrong with us? Father acts like a madman, and you . . . "

Suddenly Hun dreaded Samdŭk's answer. He stepped through the gate and walked past the fence where they were working. Perhaps he could prevent Samdŭk from answering. Ojaknyŏ rose, as if to say something, then sat down again. Samdŭk continued binding the stalks together in silence. He looked just like his father from the side.

Samdŭk was already a strong lad two years ago when Hun returned to the village. That first spring Hun decided to try growing his own rice. He couldn't depend on the tenants, who could barely fulfill their grain quotas to the government.

For the first time in his life Hun prepared a rice bed. He planted seedlings and stayed up late into the night to make sure the water was flowing properly. It was backbreaking work every step of the way, but it amounted to little more than pretense. If it hadn't been for Ojaknyŏ and Samdŭk he wouldn't have gotten anything done. Countless times he watched with wonder and admiration as the woman and boy labored in the paddies. He had never realized what it meant to work the soil.

They harvested the rice in the fall. The grain quota was heavier than the previous year. Local officials and policemen came around to search the villagers' houses and yards. They dug through piles of dried rice stalks and dragged away sacks of rice they found buried in the snow or under kitchen floors.

Hun didn't know what to do. They had harvested less than their quota. Samdŭk came over in the middle of the night to discuss where to hide the grain. Ojaknyŏ suggested hiding it under the large condiment jars in the shed. Without a word Samdŭk heaved a sack of unhulled rice onto his back and carried it into the backyard. He had always been a quiet boy. Hun trusted him all the more for his reserve. They hid five sacks of unthreshed rice down the well.

Those who fell short of their quota were summoned to the police station. Samdŭk went in Hun's place since everyone knew Samdŭk did the actual cultivating and threshing.

Samdŭk told the police that they had submitted everything they harvested. The chief of police ordered him to take off his shoes and socks and began beating the soles of his feet with an iron rod. One of the villagers, called to the station for the same offense, told Samdŭk to scream to earn their pity, but the seventeen-year-old didn't utter a single groan. Only his eyes, which grew redder and redder with each stroke of the rod, registered the pain.

Hun couldn't bear sitting at home, so he went to the police station, prepared to submit the rice they had hidden in the well. He had heard that landlords in some villages made friends with the police to avoid paying the increased quotas. He had never even been near the police station, however.

When he arrived at the station, Ojaknyŏ ran up and grabbed him by the sleeve. From the police station came the sound of flogging. Ojaknyŏ shuddered at every stroke. Her eyes grew redder and redder, too. Hun tried to enter the station, but she refused to let go of his sleeve. Her hands shook violently.

They returned home, supporting Samdŭk between them. He couldn't walk for three days. Over the next year, as Hun ate soggy rice hulled in the mortar, his throat tightened at the thought of Samdŭk's loyalty. He vowed to trust Samdŭk even more than his father had trusted Samdŭk's father. But now Samdŭk was spying on him!

When Hun awakened to his surroundings, he found himself beside Dragon Head Stream, which fed the village rice paddies. Recently he had been having this experience quite often. He would awake from his musings to find himself doing something completely unexpected. Today he had set out for the hill behind the village, but had strayed to the fields instead.

The stream took its name from the hill, shaped like a dragon's head, which stood at its source. On one bank were half a dozen willow trees, on the other a sand bar. The stream was still frozen along the bank shaded by the willows. Now and then the sound of breaking glass rang through the air. The ice was melting. Some pieces sank to the bottom, others floated downstream. The smaller ones melted before they had a chance to float away.

Hun tried to guess where the ice would break next, but each time he focused on one spot, the ice would crackle apart in another.

Suddenly something caught his eye. He leaned forward for a closer look. It was a willow branch, wrapped in ice. The branch was covered with catkins. The catkins were encased in ice as well, but one by one they thawed the ice around them. Hun's heart warmed at the sight of the tiny buds, not yet fully formed, that melted the ice surrounding them.

The field beyond the brook was a bleak expanse, still caught in winter's grip. At the far end, however, something wafted upward like the shimmering haze of spring. It was a fire the village children had lit in play.

Hun closed his eyes, and the memory of a long-forgotten grassfire wafted up in his heart as well. He must have been seven or eight at the time. It happened before his family had moved to Pyongyang, in early spring. He and some other boys his age had been amusing themselves by setting small grassfires on the hill leading to the tavern. It was great fun watching the grass blaze and stamping out the fire when it began to spread. But then, one of the fires refused to go out, no matter how hard they stamped. It would die out for an instant, then flare up again when they walked away. They began beating the ground with their jackets. This only spread the fire further.

The boys got scared and began running away one by one. In the end, Hun was all alone. He thought of running away too, but then, Ojaknyŏ appeared. She threw down her basket of wild greens and began rolling on the ground. After extinguishing one patch of burning grass, she ran to the next and rolled on it. Soon the fire was out.

Hun stood watching in amazement. And when the fire was out, he was again amazed. He saw something in Ojaknyŏ's eyes. "Your eyes are on fire!" he exclaimed.

She rubbed her eyes. "Your eyes are burning inside," he said. It was true. That was when Hun discovered Ojaknyŏ's eyes.

With his own eyes still shut, Hun recalled another encounter with those burning eyes. It happened a few years after his family moved to Pyongyang. Hun came to spend summer vacation with his grandparents.

He was relaxing on the sand bar beside the stream, soaking up the heat from the sand he had piled in a mound around himself. In those days he was young and unafraid of the blazing sun.

Suddenly, he smelled the scent of ripe melons mingling with the smell of the hot sand. He opened his eyes and looked around. There was nothing there. He closed his eyes again, but the sweet smell of melons kept wafting over him. He turned around and found two dark green melons right behind his head.

He knew who had brought them. Ojaknyŏ was standing on the bank of the stream, her baby brother strapped to her back. When their eyes met, she dashed off. For a fleeting second he saw her eyes. They were on fire.

He picked up one of the melons and bit into it. Juice filled his mouth with the sweetness of honey, then spread through his body. Even now, as he stood on the bank of the stream, his eyes still closed, it seemed as if he could smell that sweet fragrance, and see Ojaknyŏ's burning eyes.

Hun opened his eyes and looked around. He was startled to find Ojaknyŏ standing behind him.

"Oh, I didn't hear you come. How long have you been there?"

"You looked like you were thinking . . . " Ojaknyŏ said apologetically.

Lately Hun was often startled by the slightest thing, but it was different this time. His surprise bordered on a feeling of rapture today. He felt as if that incident from his childhood had some direct connection with the present. He sought her eyes, but she kept them lowered as she spoke. "Squire Yun's come to see you."

He turned to go, then paused. "Come here for a minute, won't you?"

She came closer.

"Look at those catkins. They are thawing the ice around them. It's almost as if they had warmth in their fur."

She looked at the willow branch, then broke off a wand. As she did so, the blush in her cheeks deepened to a peach red, as if the spring breeze had brought out their color.

"These paddies used to be dry fields, didn't they?" Hun asked as he stepped onto the footpath that ran between the paddies. "I think they planted melons in this one, and that one over there too."

The fields had been converted to rice paddies after the irrigation cooperative was established.

Melons. Melons so green they were almost black . . . That soft, smooth feeling . . . that tinglingly sweet fragrance . . . that juicy orange flesh . . . Hun thought of the melons that she had secretly placed beside him that day. He had eaten many melons since then, but never had he tasted any as fragrant and delicious.

"Oh, you always were fond of melons," she said pensively, as she trailed along several steps behind him. Was she thinking of that time, too?

"Yes, they're my favorite summer fruit. But they don't taste the same anymore." Perhaps he wanted to say people had changed, too, just like the fields and the color and flavor of melons.

"Sir," Ojaknyŏ said, a little hesitantly, "Please forgive him."

Hun looked back at her.

She dropped her head even lower. "Samdŭk, I mean. He's not that kind of boy. I asked him why he did it, but he wouldn't say. I told him never to do anything like that again. Please forgive him . . . just this once."

"What's there to forgive? It's not his fault. It's the times. . . ."

"He'll never do it again. He's not that kind of boy."

Hun didn't quite share her faith in him.

"I know Father's changed, but not Samdŭk."

"Don't worry about that. It's time you started thinking about your own affairs. I hear your husband's back." He was relieved to finally have a chance to broach the topic.

"Don't worry about me, sir. I've made up my mind already."

"Of course, if I just left, that would take care of the

---

problem, but somehow, I don't feel I can leave right now. It's not the land. I'll go if they tell me to, but I don't want to leave until I have to. That doesn't mean you have to stay with me, though. I've never regarded you as an estate agent's daughter and myself a landlord. Besides, those relationships don't exist anymore. You don't need to feel bound to me out of some outdated sense of loyalty."

"Sir, I didn't come to keep house for you because you were the landlord. . . . I know this sounds impertinent but . . . please don't tell me to go away. Let me look after you while you're here."

"I don't think that would be good for you."

"I don't care what happens to me. Just let me stay with you." She had been wanting to say this to him for a long time. Her heart had pounded whenever she thought of making that declaration, and now that she had made it, she felt a weight had been lifted from her.

The call of a cuckoo rang through the trees. Ojaknyŏ looked up. It came from the direction of Maiden Rock. Her heart felt like it was brimming over. She was so happy compared to the maiden in the legend.

Suddenly, she felt a shiver run down her spine. She put her hands to her cheeks. She felt as if she were getting a fever. She had been racked by fever the night before. Her face gradually turned a deep red. The hand that held the willow wand trembled.

She ignored it, though. What does a cold matter? she thought.

Squire Yun was waiting beside his oxcart, felt hat in hand.

"You should have waited inside," said Hun.

"How have you been?" Yun asked, pressing Hun's hand between his own warm, fleshy palms.

"I'm fine. Are you on your way to Pyongyang?"

Squire Yun used the oxcart for his trips to Pyongyang. He rode it as far as Sunan, where he boarded the train. The oxcart met him there on his return. He sometimes dropped in on Hun on his way.

"No, I came to see you today."

Yun had been one of his father's closest friends, so Hun naturally treated him as an uncle.

The oxcart driver handed a small package to Ojaknyŏ.

"They'd run out of liquor in my village. So I brought only a small chicken."

"Oh, you needn't have," Hun replied.

Yun turned to the oxcart driver. "You go on to Sunan and have the ox shod." Then, to Hun, "I hear they always have liquor in the tavern here. Looks like you're having some work done on your fence. Why don't we go out and have a drink?"

"As you wish, sir."

Yun seemed to have second thoughts, though. "Maybe it's not such a good idea to go out drinking nowadays. How about sending out for some and having a drink here? Then we can have a quiet chat."

Ojaknyŏ welcomed the suggestion. She didn't like the idea of Hun going out drinking. She prepared the chicken, put it on the stove, and left for the tavern. When she reached the top of the hill overlooking the tavern, she paused. Should I buy two quarts, or will one quart do? She looked down at the wine kettle in her hand. It would hold two quarts, but one quart would do. It will have to. After all, Mr. Pak isn't well.

Ojaknyŏ quickened her pace. She had closed the draft on the stove, but she was afraid the pot might boil over while she was away.

It was still early, but the tavern appeared to have some customers already. "Ma'am?" she called out softly for Pulch'ul's mother, who ran the tavern. "Are you in?"

The door swung open. A cloud of cigarette smoke hung over the room, and she couldn't see inside. Then suddenly, a man's face leaped out at her from the murky darkness. She felt dizzy; a fog even thicker than the cigarette smoke rose before her eyes. The man sprang up. "Why, look who's here!" he exclaimed. "How are you?"

Ojaknyŏ stared at him blankly.

"Well, speak of the devil! I was just talking about you. So, how have you been? How's the new marriage going? Just look at you! Come to buy liquor for your new husband! What a devoted wife! You slut! Have you forgotten that your lawful husband's still alive?"

The man grabbed the door frame, as if he to propel himself toward her, when Pulch'ul's mother caught his leg.

"Let me go. Her husband's still alive and she's off screwing another man! You whore! I ought to run you through with my knife. Hey, let go! I'm going to give it to her right this minute!"

"Calm down! You can talk when you're sober."

"What? I'm not drunk. You know, I'm a man, too. What am I supposed to do—just stand by and watch someone steal my wife? You slut, did you shack up with Pak for his money? Well, his money's useless now! Things have changed. Yeah, I'm going to kill him first! Now let go of my leg!"

Another man stood up. It was Hŭngsu. "Hey, Comrade Ch'oe! Come back and sit down," he said.

"Why, don't you agree? So what if Pak had some money in the past? We're all equal now, aren't we?"

"Now, now, comrade Ch'oe, relax and come back to the table." Hŭngsu pulled him by the sleeve.

Ch'oe returned to his seat with exaggerated reluctance. "All right, if you say so. I'll leave it for now, but just wait till I get my hands on those two!"

During the final years of colonial rule, Ch'oe had worked under Hŭngsu, who was then a construction supervisor on the irrigation project. Hŭngsu had been a difficult superior. Ch'oe had to kiss up to him, buying him presents and treating him to drinks in order to keep his job.

Things had changed, though. First of all, Hŭngsu no longer addressed him in the familiar form,* and was now buying *him* drinks. Ch'oe could hardly ignore Hŭngsu's intervention.

"Well then, give us some more wine," Ch'oe demanded.

Pulch'ul's mother looked at Hŭngsu to see if it was all right.

"Give our comrade some more wine."

"Really, she owes you her life, sir. If it hadn't been for you, I'd . . . "

"Don't call me sir. Call me comrade."

"How could I? You'll always be 'sir' to me. Really, if it hadn't been for you, I'd have finished them both off already."

"I understand how you feel, but in the future, their fate will be in your hands."

---

*The familiar form is one of the two commonly used Korean speech forms. You cannot utter a Korean sentence without indicating in what regard you hold your addressee. Korean forms of speech are divided roughly into the honorific (polite) and the plain (or familiar) forms, but there are several shades of each, produced by varying the endings of predicate parts and using different case-endings for nouns. Mastering the speech forms poses great difficulties not only for foreigners learning Korean but also for present-day Koreans whose education has not emphasized the paramount importance of using appropriate forms of address for each and every situation.

"I'm going to have it out with that Pak! And soon, believe me!"

On her way home, Ojaknyŏ wondered how she managed
to get out with her quart of liquor. She felt feverish, but told
herself to be firm. Her trials had only just begun.

She remembered the pot she had left on the stove. Now
all she could think of was getting home as quickly as possible. And she thanked God that Mr. Pak hadn't gone to the
tavern that day.

They say the Americans have come as far north as
Sariwŏn." Squire Yun's eyes grew redder with each cup of
liquor. "I heard they'll soon be pushing up to Hwangju and
Pyongyang. Did you hear that?"

"I rather doubt it. It's probably just a rumor spread by
people who'd like to see it happen," Hun responded.

"Hmm . . . " Beads of perspiration stood on Yun's pockmarked nose. "You know, they say that after land reform,
they'll let a landowner keep the land he cultivates himself."

"I heard they're confiscating all the big landowners'
holdings."

"How do they distinguish between big landowners and
small ones?"

"I think we both qualify as big landowners."

Yun owned considerable land in Chin'gol.

"Well, I've heard they'll confiscate all the absentee
landlords' holdings but leave the others enough land to cultivate on their own."

Squire Yun, however, was an absentee landlord. Several
years ago he had sold his house in the country at a cheap
price and moved to Pyongyang to speculate in real estate.
Hun had heard rumors that Yun had reaped quite a windfall
thanks to the new housing plan in Pyongyang. Only at

threshing time could his squat form and felt hat be seen swaying atop the oxcart as he traveled back and forth along the road to Sunan.

"To tell you the truth," Yun continued, his pockmarked nose even redder now. "I've got this arrangement . . . I've worked out this system with Song, my oxcart driver, so it looks like I've been cultivating some of the land myself. Do you think it'll work?"

Hun now understood why Yun had been spending so much time in his village lately.

"What's your uncle going to do?" Yun asked cautiously. He would have liked to discuss the problem with Yongje, Hun's uncle, but the two men had been on bad terms for several years now. They'd had a disagreement over water rights.

Hun's uncle also owned a considerable amount of land in Chin'gol. It was mostly dry fields, but two years ago he began converting it into rice paddies and started to build a reservoir to feed the paddies. As most of Yun's land lay below Yongje's, he would have trouble irrigating his paddies if a reservoir were built upstream. Naturally, a quarrel had resulted. This happened toward the end of the colonial period when the Japanese were anxious to increase agricultural production, so Yongje could easily obtain government support for his project. And even if he hadn't received the government's backing, he would have surely pushed the project through, for he was the kind of person who never gave up once he had set his heart on something. Squire Yun had not set foot in Hun's uncle's house since the quarrel.

"I bet your uncle's figured a way around land reform," Yun ventured.

"I rather doubt it," said Hun.

Disappointed by Hun's vague reply, Yun asked, "What are *you* going to do?"

"I have no plans. I'm just going to wait and see."

"Wait and see? What's to see? They'll drive you out, penniless."

"If they drive me out, I have no choice but to go."

Yun's eyes flashed. "What! How can you . . . Your father wouldn't have stood around wringing his hands. He'd have done something. It's no crime to be a landlord. Why, we give the tenants fertilizer and grain if they run out before the harvest. We get our rents, of course, but we're providing the tenants their livelihood. If it hadn't been for landlords like us, they'd have all starved long ago. What kind of law is it that takes away a man's property because he's been generous all his life? They're just a bunch of scoundrels." Yun's hand shook visibly as he lifted his wine cup.

Hun too was disgusted with the whole situation, though not so much at the prospect of losing his land as at the thought of the divisions that would result if land reform was carried out before the country had time to stabilize.

It was already getting dark. The kettle was empty. Ojaknyŏ peeked in from the kitchen and asked if they would like their dinner. Yun said he wasn't hungry but asked her to feed the oxcart driver if he was back from Sunan. The driver had already eaten, she replied.

"Well, I guess I'd better be going, then." Yun picked up his hat.

"Why don't you stay and have another drink? It's been so long since we last met."

"No, I've had enough."

Hun felt sorry that he wasn't able to offer his guest any comfort. He must have been in dire need of reassurance to have sought out Hun like this. The compact little man usually kept his worries to himself.

Squire Yun climbed into the oxcart and tipped his hat as he pulled away. The ox seemed to move with more confidence, thanks to its new shoes. Yun's squat frame swayed back and forth. The evening sun hit him in the eyes. He turned his head to the side and raised one hand to block the sun, looking rather forlorn. Feeling a little sad, Hun stood at the gate watching long after the oxcart had disappeared past the crossroads.

"Somebody's looking for you," a voice said. Hun turned to find Tangson pointing behind him. Hun saw no one, though.

"He went up the hill."

"Who is it?" Ojaknyŏ asked, hurrying toward them.

"I don't know. I was coming down with this firewood and some man asked me to tell Mr. Pak that he wants to talk to him."

Ojaknyŏ's face flushed dark red. When Hun disappeared around the back of the house, she ran to her brother and whispered, "Hurry up the hill! Something might happen to Mr. Pak! Please hurry!"

Samdŭk hadn't finished the fence yet.

"Oh, please, hurry!"

Samdŭk tied the panel of millet stalks to a post and cut the straw rope with his teeth. "Why are you so jumpy these days?" he grumbled.

A tall, athletic-looking man was standing on the path leading up the hill. When Hun approached, the man said, "You must be Mr. Pak. I'm sorry to trouble you." Tossing his cigarette aside, he added, "I'm Ojaknyŏ's husband."

This was bound to happen, Hun thought.

"I'd like to talk to you for a moment," the man said.

"All right. Shall we go down to my house?"

"No, I'd rather we talked somewhere else."

"Well then, let's go over there," Hun said, pointing to the old tomb. He realized it would be embarrassing for the man to come to his house.

"Let's go to the tavern and have a drink," the man suggested with a smile, his white teeth flashing between his ruddy lips.

Ojaknyǒ's husband struck a fine figure, tall and manly with a straight, well-sculpted nose. Hun took an immediate liking to him. The man kept silent as they walked up the mountain path to the tavern. He didn't seem the slightest bit drunk. Hun felt clearheaded too, although he had drunk quite a bit already.

Pulch'ul's mother panicked when she saw Hun walk in with Ch'oe. "Oh, you should have slept it off instead of coming for more," she chided.

Ch'oe glared at her. "What're you talking about? Who says I'm drunk? Now be a nice lady and bring us some wine."

She wanted to protest but held her peace. This was the man who had turned her eldest son, Pulch'ul, into a gambler. Ch'oe used to drag Pulch'ul to gambling joints in Sunan, Yǒngyu and Hanch'ǒn. She had taken him to task for it many times. She had even picked fights with him and ripped his shirt on a number of occasions. So, for a time Ch'oe had avoided the feisty woman.

Then three years before liberation, he disappeared. It had been rumored he was in jail, but there was no further news of him, even after liberation.

Then he reappeared a couple of days ago, none the worse for his experience, it seemed. And he drank as much as before.

She could hardly adopt the same tone with him now, though, because the others treated him so differently. For example, Hŭngsu, who used to bully him in the old days, now bought him drinks and used a more polite form of address. Struck once again by how the world had changed, Pulch'ul's mother thought she would have to treat him with a little more respect. She had to be especially careful these days, because of what her son had done. It was thanks to Hŭngsu's protection that she still had the tavern.

When they had almost finished their first bottle, Ch'oe lifted his bloodshot eyes to the proprietress. "Do you know where I've been all this while?" he asked.

In jail, like everyone's been saying, she thought to herself, but replied with a forced smile: "How should I know?"

"Look at this," Ch'oe said, and rolled up his left sleeve. There was a large scar, clearly a knife wound, above the elbow. "Can't you guess? I've been working in a gold mine. Yes, a gold mine. The Hoech'ang Gold Mine in Sŏngch'ŏn. Boy, it was great! I worked in a coal mine once, but that's no place for a human being. You get so dirty—no better than a mole. But a gold mine—now that's the place for a man. First of all, it makes you feel so grand! Everywhere you look, there's gold! I was promoted to foreman after a while, but in a gold mine even the lowliest miner can have all the drinks and girls he wants. Why, there was plenty of booze, even in the final days of the war when you couldn't find liquor anywhere. Women too. Loads of them. And you know what? I had a thing going with a pretty tavern girl. You know what I mean?"

In the old days when Ch'oe hung around with her son, he had addressed Pulch'ul's mother as Mother. It irritated her that he should chat with her in such a patronizing tone now, but she saw no need to rub him the wrong way. "Oh, I'm sure all the girls were wild for you," she replied prudently.

"Well, not exactly. My reputation's pretty bad. But, you know what? Pulch'ul wouldn't have gotten into that trouble if I'd been around. I'd have saved him from falling into traps. Now, how about one more bottle?"

"I think you've had enough for today. And Mr. Pak can't drink much . . . "

"What're you talking about? I've heard he's quite a drinker. Right, sir? How could we become friends so quickly if we weren't such hearty drinkers? Don't you agree, sir?"

Hun wished the man would hurry up and get drunk enough to come out and say what he had to say.

Ch'oe glared at Pulch'ul's mother. "Come on, bring some more wine. I don't drink on credit any more, if that's what you're worried about."

"I'll be all right. Bring us one more bottle," Hun said.

A small boy of four or five sat staring at them full of curiosity. Ch'oe asked him to bring a couple of dried pollacks, and began softening them by pounding them against the tavern's millstone.

Pulch'ul's mother brought them more wine, praying to herself that nothing would happen. She was uneasy, having seen how the man had treated Ojaknyŏ earlier in the day.

Ch'oe drank silently for some time, then began hiccuping. "Er . . . hic . . . Why am I hiccupping all of a sudden? Hic . . . They say you can get the hiccups from stealing . . . Maybe it's 'cause I forced you to give me this wine. Hic . . . Well, Mr. Pak, why don't we go out and get some air? Hic . . . Ma'am, how much do I owe you?"

At last, Hun thought.

Ch'oe staggered to his feet and began fishing through his pockets. "Well, ma'am . . . I'm afraid you'll have to put that on my bill."

Hun took some money from his pocket and started counting.

"Oh, no. Hic . . . I'll take care of this, sir. I'll pay tomorrow," Ch'oe said, brushing Hun's hand away. But then, he seemed to change his mind. "Well, ma'am, hic . . . Take your money. That's what's so nice about drinking buddies. Hic . . . whoever has the money pays, even if they've never met before! Hic . . ."

They stepped outside. The evening mist had settled over the valley already. Ch'oe stepped around the corner of the tavern and urinated, then wobbled up to Hun and put his arm around his shoulders. Hun thought he saw Ch'oe's other hand move. He's going to throttle me, he thought.

But Ch'oe simply walked, his arm around Hun still. "Hic . . . I'm sorry about the bill. I let you pay 'cause I didn't want to refuse your hospitality. Hic . . . But what's the big deal? I could have paid her later. Hic . . . By the way, do you know who made it possible for her to hold onto that tavern after what her son did? Hic . . . Hŭngsu. Yes, I said, Hŭngsu. Hic . . . Now this is just between you and me. Do you know whose little boy that is? Hic . . . Hŭngsu's. Yeah, she has five kids . . . Hic . . . and they all have different fathers. Hic . . . Hŭngsu was mighty powerful when he was supervisor on that irrigation project. People took him out drinking every night. Hic . . . I treated him often enough myself when I was working for him. And you know what? He likes snake soup. Yeah, I caught a fair number of snakes for him myself. Hic . . . but he's changed . . . ever since he became chairman of the youth committee. He's gotten so polite. Why, he treats me almost like an equal, you know."

Ch'oe stopped when they were halfway down the hill and withdrew his arm from Hun's shoulders. "Hic . . . please forgive me. Why, I'm doing all the talking. Hic . . . I wonder where I got these hiccups from? Hic . . . Actually, there was something I wanted to talk to you about."

Hun felt Ch'oe's hot breath on his face.

"You can guess what it's about, can't you? I wanted to make things clear between us." His hiccups were gone now. "People think Ojaknyŏ couldn't stand living with me 'cause of my debauchery, but that's not true. Sure, I've sown some wild oats in my time, but not while I was married to her. I might as well tell you everything. It's not that I disliked her or neglected her. She's a good-looking girl, though her eyes are a bit strong for a woman. In fact, I rather liked her eyes. Anyway, I didn't throw her out 'cause I didn't like her. But she had this strange way about her. I couldn't take it. She never let me touch her above the waist. From the wedding night on, she kept her bosom wrapped up so tight I couldn't get near it. At first I thought she was just shy. But that wasn't it. She never let me touch her breasts. That's when I started beating her . . . to teach her a lesson. But no matter how hard I hit her, she wouldn't let me near her breasts. Then I realized she must have another man in her heart, so I just beat the life out of her and sent her packing. I told her to go live with the guy, whoever it was. So you see? It's not that I didn't like her . . . And now that I think about it, I realize you must be the one."

Hun looked the man in the eye.

"You're wrong."

"Wrong? You mean you're going to deny it?" He drew a sharp breath.

"There's nothing between your wife and me."

"Even though you've been living under the same roof for the last three years?"

"I swear on my honor that Ojaknyŏ is as pure as she was the day she left you."

Ch'oe's red eyes glared at Hun for a while, then he spoke. "I thought I'd beat you to a pulp the moment we met, but once I saw how frail you were, I couldn't bring myself to use force on you. I'd heard you could drink, though, so I figured we could share a couple of drinks and talk frankly, man to man. I may not have much of an education, but I know how a man should act. If only you'll be honest with me, I'd give you my wife!"

"I told you the truth. You can take your wife back whenever you like."

"All right, I'll come for her tomorrow."

That night, though relieved by Hun's safe return, Ojaknyŏ was feverish and couldn't sleep. The next morning she still had a temperature. She cooked breakfast as usual, though. Hun noticed she was flushed when she brought in the breakfast tray.

"You look as if you've got a temperature," he remarked.

"Oh, it's nothing," she said, lowering her eyes.

"Take this and get back into bed after breakfast," he said, wrapping a few aspirin tablets in a piece of paper. Ch'oe said he'd come for her today, so she'd better get well before he arrives, Hun thought.

He considered telling her that her husband was coming to fetch her, but he decided against it. She had told him that her mind was already made up about her future. It was up to them to decide what to do. All he could do was stay out of their way so they could talk it over freely.

He went up to the old tomb site. A magpie alighted on a twig in front of him, flapped its wings several times as if to shake off some weight, then flew away. Visible through the bushes was a throng of people passing along the road. It was the funeral procession for Kwŏn. There were several paper banners, and the bier was quite sumptuous.

Suddenly he heard footsteps behind him.

"Oh, there you are!" It was Hŭngsu. "Are you expecting Ch'oe today?" he asked.

"Yes," Hun said.

"Well, I ran into him on the road just now. He asked me to tell you that he'll be back in a couple of days. He said he had some urgent business in Sunan. Something about renting a house."

Ch'oe would be welcome to live in my house if Ojaknyŏ decided to take him back, Hun thought.

"And I must warn you. He's a rough character. Be careful! Well then, good day to you!" Hŭngsu hurried off, probably to catch up with the funeral procession. Then he retraced his steps. "Er, there's one other thing," he said, glancing around warily. "Squire Yun came to see you yesterday, didn't he? Don't tell anyone I said this, but it'd be better if you didn't have anything to do with the likes of him from now on." Hŭngsu sounded as if he was giving Hun an important piece of advice, and from his tone, Hun had no difficulty imagining what Hŭngsu's job as chairman of the youth committee entailed.

The widow was sitting with her back to the mourners, some distance from the newly dug grave. She didn't seem to be crying; her head and shoulders were still. She rose when the men began lowering the coffin into the ground, and looked around nervously, as if searching for someone. Her bloodshot eyes were the only sign of her distress. She walked over to the young man in the dog-fur coat.

"Sir, can you give me some of Myŏnggu's father's land, like you said? I know I told you I didn't want anything, land or money, but now that I think about it . . . how am I going to raise those kids? Just give me the paddy land down by the mudflat and that field on the western slope. We can make a living off that, even after rent. Myŏnggu's family has other land, so they'll be all right. And I'll pay them a share of the harvest, just like any other tenant. I'm not after a handout. I don't want to exchange my husband's life for land."

The young man scowled. This comrade is sadly lacking in revolutionary spirit, he thought.

4

Ojaknyŏ took to her bed in the end. She had tried the aspirin and wrapping herself up in a quilt but the fever burned on. She wasn't going to allow herself to give in to something as trivial as a cold, and since work was the best remedy for such ailments, she had set about doing her chores in the kitchen. But after several dizzy spells, she finally asked her mother to look after the house for a day and took to her bed.

Hun went to Dr. Kim and asked him to make a house call.

"I'm sure it's just influenza," the doctor said. "It's quite common in early spring, you know. I'll give you some medicine."

"Aspirin doesn't seem to work."

"Well then, I'll give you something stronger."

Hun returned home with three packets of powdered medicine. Ojaknyŏ took it as instructed, but her fever did not improve. Hun returned to the doctor the following day. "Won't you please come and take a look at her?"

The doctor hesitated, then agreed. "I'll be right over. You go on ahead."

Hun waited and waited but the doctor didn't appear. More than two hours had passed when he heard a quiet tap on the door. It was Doctor Kim. Hun asked him in, but the doctor said he was busy and went straight to the patient's room.

A short time later there was another knock on the door. Declining Hun's repeated invitation to come inside, the doctor simply said, "I was right, it *is* influenza. And a bit of an upset stomach as well. I gave her a shot. She should be up and around in no time."

Her fever showed no sign of subsiding, however. Something about Ojaknyŏ's illness bothered Hun. It didn't seem like an ordinary cold or simple fatigue. They couldn't wait around doing nothing without knowing what the illness was, so Hun returned to the doctor's late that afternoon.

Dr. Kim ran his hand over his bald pate. "That's strange," he said. "I expected her to be better by now. Why don't we wait a while and see?"

"Please come and examine her one more time. It looks serious to me," Hun said. He handed the doctor a wad of bills, more than enough to cover the cost of a house call.

"All right, I'll be there shortly."

But the doctor didn't come. Hun assumed that a more serious case had arisen. The following morning as Hun prepared to go looking for him, Dr. Kim appeared at his door, in a great hurry it seemed. He didn't even have his medical bag.

Hun stood outside Ojaknyŏ's room and waited for the examination to finish. He heard a reedy whistling sound. A tiny leaf on the new millet stalk fence was vibrating in the wind. It must have escaped trimming somehow. Hun hadn't noticed a breeze, but the leaf whistled all the same. He walked over and plucked it in irritation. The doctor emerged soon after, wiping his palms with a piece of cotton soaked in alcohol.

"She has quite a temperature, doesn't she?" Hun asked in a whisper.

"It's typhoid fever."

"Typhoid fever?" Hun's heart sank. That's what his mother had died of.

"The rash has already begun to appear around her mouth. It'll spread over her body soon."

"Is there any treatment?"

"Well, she has to stay in bed, and you should keep applying cold compresses to her forehead. The fever will probably peak tomorrow. She mustn't give in to the fever, otherwise . . ."

Hun knew there was no treatment. His mother died when her heart gave out during the fever.

"And, you know, typhoid is most infectious when the rash starts to disappear. So be especially careful then." Dr. Kim ran his hand over his bald forehead several times, then hurried off as if to another urgent patient. He paused after a few steps, though, and turned to look at Hun.

"Now that we know what she has, I won't be coming again. After all, there's nothing more I can do."

Hun thought of asking him to come and give her a heart stimulant from time to time, but he refrained from doing so. He understood what the doctor was saying. Dr. Kim didn't want to be seen at Hun's house. That was why he hadn't entered Hun's room on his first visit, and why he had broken his promise the day before. He hadn't even brought his medical bag today. Maybe he carried the syringes in his pocket so no one would guess where he was going.

Steam rose from Dr. Kim's bald pate as he passed through the gate. He clearly wouldn't be visiting again.

Ojaknyŏ is risking her life by staying with me, Hun thought. He had never felt so anxious in his life.

Ojaknyŏ's mother couldn't look after her daughter properly. Tosŏp had forbidden her from going to Hun's house.

"She's not my daughter anymore," he had declared. "I don't care what happens to her, and if I catch anyone going over to see her, I'll beat the living daylights out of them!"

The poor woman was terrified. When her husband wasn't watching, she would sneak over to Hun's house to peek in on Ojaknyŏ, then steal away without a word. She was sure her daughter would die with no one to nurse her, and her cheeks were wet with tears from morning to night.

Hun began to apply cold compresses to Ojaknyŏ's forehead, though she insisted he needn't bother. She felt guilty and embarrassed at the thought of being a burden to him.

As he sat beside her, preparing fresh compresses, Hun stared at a pine knot he had discovered at the bottom of the sliding door. It caught the sunlight and let off a strangely transparent glow, a reddish color, but what kind of red was it? The more he looked at it, the more beautiful it seemed. The color reminded him of a flower, but he couldn't think of its name. A wild rose? A pomegranate blossom?

Hun did the cooking as well, but Ojaknyŏ ate little. She tried some gruel, for Hun's sake if nothing else, but she could hardly swallow it.

Kim Pokdong's wife came to look in on her. She entered the house through the kitchen, stuck her head in Ojaknyŏ's room, clucked a few times, and quietly closed the door again. Ojaknyŏ asked who it was, without opening her eyes, and Hun told her Pokdong's wife had come to check on her.

Ojaknyŏ's bloodshot eyes popped open. She sat up and looked through the glass panel in the sliding door. She slid the door open and called out. "Mrs. Kim!"

Pokdong's wife had already reached the front gate. "Oh, I heard you were sick so I came to see you. Hurry up and get well."

"What's that?"

"What do you mean?"

"What's that hidden in your skirt?"

"Oh, it's nothing."

"Let's see!"

"I told you, it's nothing."

"Nothing? Bring it here and show me!"

The woman removed her hand from the folds of her skirt. She was holding a brass bowl.

"See! I'm just borrowing a bowl."

"Did you ask?"

"Oh come on! What's the big deal? It's just a bowl."

"How could you stoop so low? Bring it here, right now!"

"Why're you making such a fuss? I heard they're going to seize this house and everything in it any day now. What's so bad about taking one little bowl before they come?"

"Where did you hear such a thing? No one's going to touch a thing in this house as long as I'm alive!"

"Greedy girl! You mean, you're going to keep it all to yourself? Don't be such a pig."

"Are you going to do as I say or not?" Ojaknyŏ wobbled over the threshold onto the veranda.

"All right! Keep it all to yourself!" snapped Pokdong's wife as she flung the bowl on the ground.

"Like a crow pecking at a corpse," Ojaknyŏ murmured as she collapsed on her bedding. Hun wished she had let the poor woman keep the bowl.

The fever peaked the next day, just as the doctor had predicted. Ojaknyŏ shuddered each time Hun placed a fresh towel on her forehead. She tried to suppress her groans, but her chest heaved as she gasped for breath, then she began to rave.

"Hey, give me that bowl . . . No, you can't have that . . . not while I'm alive. Hey! What are you doing with that pot?

No, no . . . Oh, the pot's going to boil over. I've got to get back, at once." She tossed and turned. "No, you villain! No, Ch'oe! You can do what you like but don't touch my breasts! No, no, help me! Samdŭk, go see what that awful Ch'oe's doing to Mr. Pak! Please, hurry! Hurry!"

She lay still for a moment, as if to catch her breath, then heaved a great sigh and called out again. "Help! Help! Take this weight off my chest!" She ripped open the bodice of her dress and her breasts spilled out. Her fair skin was stained pink by the rash. "Help! Help! I'm dying! Some-body, please fetch an axe and split my chest open!"

Hun pulled the quilt over her breasts but Ojaknyŏ pushed it off. Her breasts heaved violently. As he pulled up the quilt again, her hand grabbed his. It burned with fever. He pulled his hand away, and it brushed against her firm breasts and hard nipples. He tucked the quilt around her shoulders, but she kicked it off again. Then she began to grab at her chest. Bloody scratch marks formed on the pink skin.

"Please, please split open my chest!"

Hun turned and looked at the pine knot. It caught the midday sun and sparkled with an iridescent light. The color was even harder to define today.

"I'm suffocating. Please, won't someone open up my chest so I can breathe?"

I have to stop her from scratching herself, Hun thought, but he was afraid of getting near those heaving breasts again. For some reason, he felt as though, simply by being there, he were defiling the purity that she had preserved for so long.

"Oh, the cuckoo's crying from Maiden Rock. The maiden's crying. Poor thing! Such a poor thing," Ojaknyŏ murmured, then she suddenly began to sob. "Mr. Pak, please don't make me leave. Please! Let me stay with you . . ."

With the approach of evening, the pine knot ceased to glow. Hun could hear rain dripping from the eaves.

Ojaknyŏ fell into a troubled sleep. She jerked awake from time to time to scream and cry. Hun felt as if the rain-laden black sky were pressing down on him.

It was two days before the fever ebbed and Hun returned to his own room. His limbs were heavy with fatigue, but his heart was light. He was grateful that she had withstood the fever and felt pleased and a bit surprised that he had nursed her so well.

He went to his desk. The willow catkins were covered with thick gray fur now. He had placed the branch that Ojaknyŏ had picked in a bottle on the desk. The bottle was almost dry.

Hun plucked a few catkins from the branch and lay down on the floor. He lined the catkins up in a row and slapped the lacquered paper floor* with his palm. The catkins hardly moved. Perhaps the floor was too hard.

As a child he had often amused himself with catkins. He lined them up on a reed mat, and when he hit it with his palm, the catkins rolled and bounced, like a litter of furry puppies. Some would only move to the side while others caught on bits of reed sticking from the mat and spun round and round. It was great fun to watch them.

---

*Rooms in traditional Korean houses have stone or cement floors, which sit on top of heating flues running the entire length of the room underneath (these are called *ondol* floors). It is a great Korean invention, thanks to which relatively few Koreans suffer from arthritis and backaches. The floors are covered with flooring paper, which are fortified and beautified by repeated coatings of lacquer or varnish and kept clean all the time. So, Koreans remove their shoes before entering the rooms, and sit and sleep on the floors.

The catkins blurred before him and his eyes began to smart. He rested his head on his arm and closed his eyes. He must have slept for some time, because the sun was streaming across the room when he awoke.

Suddenly he thought of something. It was a cluster of wild lilies growing from a crevice in a large, dark rock. His heart leaped. That was it! The pine knot on the door in Ojaknyŏ's room was the color of wild lilies.

He stepped into the kitchen and opened the door into Ojaknyŏ's room. The pine knot was glowing in the evening sun. Yes, it's the color of a wild lily, Hun whispered to himself.

Ojaknyŏ was still sleeping, lips slightly parted. Her breathing had returned to normal. Her face seemed the color of wild lilies too. Hun closed the door softly and turned to go back to his room when he saw through the glass panel of the kitchen door a form by the gate. It was Tangson. It had been a long time since he had paid Tangson's grandfather a visit.

After washing his face at the well, Hun slipped on his jacket and went out. Spring seemed even nearer after the rain.

As he stepped into Old Ko's yard, Hun heard Tangson crying inside the house. It sounded as if the boy was being beaten by his grandfather. Having seen the boy only moments before, Hun wondered why. He pulled on the door handle, but it was latched from inside.

"May I come in? It's me, Hun."

The sound of the old man's switch stopped, and Tangson's cries lapsed to a quiet whimper. "Is someone out there?" a breathless voice asked.

"Yes, sir. It's me, Hun."

"Oh, is that you?" the old man responded, but the door didn't open. The sound of the switch resumed, as did the cries of pain. Between screams the boy pleaded, "Forgive me, Grandpa. Please forgive me this once!" Then he seemed to collapse on the floor. The old man ordered him to stand and take his beating again.

"Grandpa, please forgive me. I won't do it again, ever," the young voice pleaded.

"No, you must take your punishment. Stand up!"

"Why are you beating him?" Hun asked, shaking the door handle. "Please open the door."

"Just wait a minute. Now boy, stand up!" The sound of the switch and Tangson's cries began once more.

"Why are you doing this? Please calm down and let me come in," Hun pleaded.

Snap! The switch seemed to have broken. "Now, it's my turn," the old man gasped. There was a pause as he picked up a new switch, and this time the switch seemed to hit not flesh but bone.

"Grandpa, please forgive me! Please!" The boy was even more desperate now, perhaps clinging to his grandfather's arm. "Let go. Step back and watch your grandfather take his punishment. The switch is nothing compared with the pain in my heart."

Then snap! The switch broke again. The old man sobbed a few times, then silence fell over the room.

After a while, Hun heard the latch being lifted by an unsteady hand.

"Come in," the old man said, his voice trembling.

Hun couldn't see a thing when he first stepped inside, but as his eyes adjusted to the darkness, the old man's white beard came into focus and he saw the two broken switches lying on the floor in front of him. The old man stared blankly into space, while the boy sobbed in the far corner, his back to the door and face buried between his knees.

"I heard Ojaknyŏ was sick. How's she doing?" the old man asked, his eyes still staring straight ahead.

"She seems to have gotten over the worst of it."

The old man dropped his head slowly. "Actually, I have to apologize for something."

Puzzled, Hun looked at the old man in silence.

"That boy did you wrong. A big wrong."

"What are you talking about?"

"You're going to be mighty angry when you hear this." The old man paused to let out a long sigh. "You see, I was just down at the well fetching some water when I caught sight of Hŭngsu stuffing something into Tangson's pocket. When I asked the boy what was going on, he said Hŭngsu had taught him to read the inscription on the marble monument. Well, it smelled fishy to me, so I asked him what Hŭngsu had stuck in his pocket, and he said nothing at all. I knew the boy was lying. After all, I'd seen Hŭngsu putting something in his pocket! So I dragged him home and searched through his pockets. And what did I find but four ten-*won* notes. I asked him where he got the money, and he said Hŭngsu gave it to him for being a clever boy. What a story! That's why I took the switch to him. He told the truth in the end. He said Hŭngsu paid him to hang around your place and see what's going on between you and Ojaknyŏ. The bastard!" The old man's teary eyes flashed.

Hun felt a shiver running down his spine. A few days earlier Hŭngsu had told him to be on guard for Ojaknyŏ's husband and avoid the likes of Squire Yun. Obviously Hŭngsu himself was responsible for spying on him. Hun shuddered at the thought.

"Of course, Hŭngsu's the one who should be whipped,"

the old man continued angrily. "Imagine paying a boy to do something like that! Still, Tangson was wrong. It's my fault. I should have done a better job of teaching him. Please forgive me." The old man's beard quivered.

"It's nobody's fault," Hun countered. "It's all because of the times."

"Damn the times! There are things a man should and shouldn't do." The old man turned to his grandson. "Boy, you go and give that villain back his dirty money. You know what they say about squealers and spies? The grass stops growing for three years after they sit on it, 'cause even the earth hates them."

Tangson staggered to his feet. Hun took out his handkerchief and wiped the boy's eyes and nose.

"He's my only kin," the old man sighed after the boy left the room.

"He's just a child."

"But you know that old saying: Only straight shoots grow into straight trees." The old man sighed once more.

Blood oozed from the cuts on the old man's shins. His legs were covered with bruises. Hun offered his handkerchief.

"Oh, no," the old man said and picked up a handful of straw.

"That's all right. I have to wash it anyway," Hun said, and wiped the old man's legs with his handkerchief.

"I'm so ashamed," the old man said.

"Oh, don't let it upset you so. People change, you know."

"Yes, but it's much easier for a good man to go bad than for a bad man to turn good."

Hun rose to leave. It was time to cook Ojaknyŏ's gruel. The old man stood in the doorway and watched Hun leave. "Oh, did you hear?" he asked, as if something had suddenly come to mind.

"No, what?" Hun looked back.

"About tomorrow."

"I didn't hear anything."

"They say there's going to be a peasants' assembly. To enforce the new land reform . . . "

"Really?"

"What's to become of this world?"

Hun had anticipated this, and yet, for a moment, his heart was split in two. He felt as if the world around him was being broken down the middle.

After taking Ojaknyŏ a bowl of gruel and eating a few spoonfuls of rice for his own dinner, Hun began to rummage through his stationery drawers and clothes chest. Better put things in order before they come, he thought.

He found a photograph in one of the drawers. It was a picture of himself taken on his first birthday. The photographer must have rung a bell or maybe his mother had clapped her hands, for the baby was looking straight at the camera, his eyes round and wondering. The photograph was faded and yellowed but the eyes shone clearly.

The baby was so cute. It was hard to believe that he had once been such a cute baby. Hun put the photograph and several shirts in his suitcase. Then he took out the family land deeds and his father's seal and tied them in a bundle.

He found a neat pile of fabric in the chest. It was the silk dress goods his mother had purchased for his future bride. His mother had worn a ring too, he remembered. He groped around the bottom of the chest and found the ring wrapped in a piece of yellowed mulberry paper.

He took the fabric and ring to Ojaknyŏ's room. The bowl of gruel sat outside the door. She had eaten half of it today. Ojaknyŏ had pulled up the quilt to cover her face. She must be feeling embarrassed about what happened the night before.

"Ojaknyŏ, I want you to have these as a remembrance."

Ojaknyŏ sat bolt upright.

"No, just lie down. My mother bought this fabric for my wedding. Please take it."

Ojaknyŏ began to tremble all over.

"And my mother used to wear this ring. I'd like you to have it, as a remembrance of course."

"Oh, I couldn't, sir!"

"I know they're seizing all the landlords' property, but I don't think it'd be illegal for me to give you these."

"No, you must keep them for later . . ."

"I'll have no use for them, ever."

Hun thought he saw a flash in Ojaknyŏ's eyes.

"And I'd like to give you this house, too. If your husband wouldn't mind . . . I haven't heard anything of him since he went to rent a house in Sunan, though."

"No, no, never!" Ojaknyŏ collapsed, shoulders heaving, on her side. Her dark hair draped over her face.

Fearing something improper might happen, Hun rose to go, but Ojaknyŏ threw her arms around his legs. He tried to push her away, but her arms drew him closer and began climbing up his body. Her long, dark hair streamed to her waist.

"Why didn't you let me die? Why did you save me?" she cried. Her hot breath and bare breasts heaved against his chest.

He stood motionless, as if drained of all strength, his hands resting on her shoulders. Dr. Kim's words flashed through his mind. Typhoid fever is most infectious when the rash begins to disappear. "I don't want to live, either!" he murmured. "I don't want to live, either!"

Ojaknyŏ rubbed her face against his chest, then gasped and fell in a heap on the bedding. She lay perfectly still for a moment, as if she had stopped breathing, then her back heaved up and her shoulders began to jerk with convulsions. A sobbing sound filtered through the tent of dark hair.

Hun felt his blood boiling within him. But a small voice called to him from a far corner of his heart: This is wrong. You mustn't lay a finger on her. Don't move a muscle, not even to pull the quilt over her shoulders. Quick! Turn your eyes away!

He dashed from the room. Only after roaming the woods for several hours was he able to go to the crossroads and give Old Ko his father's reading glasses and Tangson his own pocket watch.

5

She must have been embarrassed by the events of the previous evening. Ojaknyŏ kept her quilt pulled over her face and didn't touch the gruel Hun had cooked for her.

The morning mist had lifted and the sun shone over the woods. It looked like it was going to be another cold, clear day.

After breakfast Hun headed for the hill where his ancestral graves were. There was a long ridge rising beyond the tavern. At its eastern tip it culminated in a cliff by Maiden Rock; to the northwest it zigzagged, revealing the raw, red earth, and gathered to form a small peak. Hun's ancestral graves were located in a pine grove on that peak.

The morning sun bathed the pines in light, but the earth remained cold and damp. Frost still covered the ground in the shade. Hun's parents were buried under a single mound. It seemed unusually large, even for a double grave. Perhaps it was because of the shadow that stretched to one side in the morning sun.

Hun placed the bundle of land deeds on the stone altar in front of the grave. He untied the string and struck a match. The dry paper burst into flames, then sputtered out in a puff of blue smoke. The papers must be packed too tightly together, Hun thought. He picked up the first deed and touched the match to it. The paper caught fire immediately and shriveled to ashes. When the first deed was gone, he lit another, then another. Soon he was warming his hands by the fire.

Through the flickering blue flames he could see words: wet paddy, 4,500 *p'yŏng*,* dry field, 2,200 *p'yŏng,* irrigated paddy, 1,300 *p'yŏng* . . . They seemed as meaningless as the numbers on the scraps of paper he and his friends used to play bank with as children.

Next came the forest land, 3.4 hectares, and building site, 1,900 *p'yŏng* . . .

Hun soon lost interest in the numbers. He crumpled the rest of the deeds and placed them in the fire. It blazed up, and he dropped his father's seal into the flames. Soon the papers were gone. Ashes danced on the breeze, and the ivory seal lay scorched and yellow on the blackened altar stone. Hun broke a twig from a pine tree and buried the seal, as if it were the bones of a cremated corpse.

He stood up and was about to take a look around the family graves before heading home when he saw a flash through the red pine trunks. A throng of people was gathering along the road which spanned the fields below. They must be from Chin'gol, Hun thought. They're coming to the peasants' assembly.

There was another flash, then another. Hun walked to the edge of the hill which overlooked the road, but he still couldn't tell where the flashes were coming from. The red dirt road coiled around the hill, revealing itself at stretches, then hiding behind the trees again. The people's legs seemed as red as the earth itself. The color gradually grew fainter on their upper bodies to become a milky white. Some people wore white kerchiefs around their heads. Those were the lightest of all.

The flashes continued. Hun realized they were all carry-

P'yŏng is the most common unit of area measurement in Korea. One *p'yŏng* is equivalent to 36 square feet or 3.24 square meters.

ing something in their hands. That's what was causing the flashing. The procession crossed the stepping-stone bridge, and as they ascended the embankment on this side of the stream, he could see the marchers' breath.

At the head of the procession was a man in a dark blue suit and combat helmet. From time to time he looked back and said something to the others. The tangled procession would pull into order at his instruction, but it wasn't long before the marchers fell out of step again.

As they drew closer, Hun could see they were carrying plowshares. Some had spades and rakes, and others carried sickles bound to long rods.

There was another flash. The sickle blades gleamed brightest. Suddenly Hun recalled what the young man in the dog-fur coat had said after Kwǒn was murdered with a sickle. *We'll avenge our comrade's murder a thousand times over, no, ten thousand times over.*

Hun spun around as if to dodge the sickle blades. His heart was pounding. And in one corner of his heart, a voice called out: "I'm not your enemy! I didn't do anything wrong!" The wind had blown the ashes away. There was nothing left on the altar stone except a sooty circle where the fire had been. It wouldn't be long before the rain washed that away, too.

Hun felt strangely relieved. And for the first time he knew he was prepared to quietly endure the wrath that might be aimed at the ancestors who lay buried in these grass-covered graves.

The peasants' assembly was held in the primary school yard. The man in the dog-fur coat paused for a moment to survey the peasants gathered before him. Then he raised his parched voice and spoke.

"All right, I'll call out the names of the reactionary land-lords one by one. It's up to you comrades to criticize them as you see fit. You are the judges today. There'll be no interference from anyone. This is a people's tribunal, a noble practice unique to the communist system."

He unfolded the paper he was holding and began to read. "Let us begin with Pak Yongje, a typical reactionary landlord who has been bleeding the peasants for many generations!"

"Yes! Down with Pak Yongje, the reactionary landlord!" shouted a man brandishing a well-polished ax. It was Tosŏp. The crowd turned to him in astonishment. Those in the back rose on tiptoe to see who had spoken. The young man on the platform glared at Tosŏp.

Tosŏp lowered his ax in haste. It seemed he had acted too soon.

The young man continued: "We all know that the reactionary landlord Pak Yongje collaborated with the Japanese colonialists. He served on the town committee under the Japanese, and toward the end of the occupation he exploited the blood and sweat of innumerable peasants on the pretext of digging a reservoir in Chin'gol. Does anybody object to branding Pak Yongje an obstacle to the democratic development of our country?"

"No! No objection! Down with the reactionary landlord Pak Yongje!" Plowshares shot up here and there, but most belonged to the party operatives who had escorted the peasants to the assembly.

Raising his ax more cautiously this time, Tosŏp turned to search the crowd for his neighbors. His eyes were full of venom. They seemed to reprimand the neighbors for failing to raise their weapons as he had instructed. When Tosŏp's eyes met theirs, Carpenter Kang and Kim Pokdong lifted their plowshares into the air.

"Comrades!" The young man continued. "Have no fear. No one's going to hamper your freedom here. Go ahead and raise your hands. If you hesitate, you could be taken for cowardly reactionaries."

More plowshares went up.

"Good! The verdict is clear." The young man nodded vigorously. "Well then, if anyone objects to branding Pak Yongje an obstacle to our democratic development, raise your hand!"

He swept his eyes across the assembly and said, "I see. No one objects. Well then, we'll proceed to Pak Hun, nephew of the reactionary landlord Pak Yongje and an evil reactionary landlord himself.

"In fact, Pak Hun is the most corrupt reactionary in Karakkol. He spends his days drinking and criticizing our democratic revolution. He is also responsible for luring ignorant young men into a reactionary band and inciting them to murder the chairman of the town peasant committee. Moreover, he has used his power as landlord to seduce the daughter of one of his tenants, a married woman at that. The wronged father and husband are here among us today."

The crowd stirred with excitement.

"Our new peasant committee chairman is the poor woman's father, and the vice-chairman of the Sunan youth committee is her husband. There is no question that Pak is a corrupt reactionary and I am certain no one will object to eliminating the evil reactionary landlord Pak Hun."

"That's right! Down with the evil reactionary Pak Hun!"

More plowshares were raised than before. Those who had hesitated at first seemed to find it easier to join the attack now.

"Next we will consider the reactionary absentee landlord Yun Kip'ung. Yun Kip'ung moved to Pyongyang seven or eight years ago to speculate on real estate and has sucked the blood of us peasants for years with his usury. This absentee landlord returned to Chin'gol some time ago and has been plotting to obstruct our democratic development ever since. For example, he has sold his land to innocent farmers destined to receive it free of charge under the land reform program, and he has bribed one of his tenants to give false testimony, ordering him to say he, Yun, has been farming land that the tenant was tilling himself. I believe all of you here would like to see this evil reactionary absentee landlord Yun Kip'ung eliminated."

"Yes! Down with the reactionary absentee landlord Yun Kip'ung!"

Even more plowshares shot up this time. The people seemed to realize they had nothing to lose, and plenty to gain, by lifting their tools.

The blades glittered beneath the blue sky. The fear and astonishment that had played on the peasants' faces earlier was gradually replaced by a look of bloodthirsty greed.

Only Song Kwanho seemed confused now. He was the tenant Squire Yun had paid to say he was cultivating the land that Song had been tilling. Yun had promised to give him the ox and cart if the plan succeeded.

Suddenly the smooth broad rump of the fatted ox flashed before Song's eyes. By hook or by crook, I'm going to make that ox mine, he thought. I'll never have a chance like this again! But then he felt a piercing stare fixed on his face. It was Comrade Shin, the party operative who had led them here this morning. Song raised his plowshare in the air as he considered what to do. Yes, I'll talk to Shin in private later on. I'll tell him the truth—that Squire Yun promised me the ox and cart if I said he was farming that land. He'll understand, and the other villagers have nothing to lose by backing my story.

Chang, another party operative who had been walking back and forth at the rear of the crowd, suddenly shouted in an angry tone. "Hey, you there with the white beard! How come you're not raising your hand? Do you have something against democratic reform?"

"I don't understand any of this," Old Ko said.

"Here, let me see your hands," the younger man demanded, snatching the old man's hand to examine his palm. "These calluses prove you've been exploited all your life. Why haven't you brought your plowshare?"

"I don't understand what any of this means."

"Don't tell me you haven't thrown off your slave's mentality!"

"I don't understand what you mean."

The young man on the platform raised his parched voice once more. "Well then, comrades, you are now courageous warriors in our campaign for democratic reform. You must now march straight to the reactionary landlords and purge them with your own hands. Once again, let me remind you: this sacred task hinges on our merciless efforts. Do not forget that for a minute. Now, let us march, each to his own village!"

The man in the helmet, who had been standing on the platform silently studying the crowd, turned to say something to the young man. He had been dispatched from the provincial peasant committee headquarters. The young man listened respectfully.

"Comrade, you have to show a little creativity."

The young man's face blanched.

"In my opinion, it would be better to divide them into two teams consisting of people from both villages. These ignorant peasants lack revolutionary consciousness. They still have strong ties to the local landlords. You won't accomplish anything without taking forceful action."

It was true. The young man's face reddened as he beckoned to his colleagues scattered through the crowd. "Comrades, form two groups, combining the contingents from Karakkol and Chin'gol."

Confusion swept the schoolyard.

The young man regretted his lack of creativity. Why hadn't he thought of that? He should have divided the peasants into two groups before the assembly began. Creativity! Yes, creativity was essential to their glorious task. He deserved to undergo self-criticism for his lack of imagination. Suddenly he was seized by panic. The provincial representative's report could decide his fate. His face blanched once again. But he couldn't give up now. He had to struggle even more valiantly, if only to make up for this blunder. Yes, he would remain in Karakkol to make certain that the reactionary landlords Pak Yongje and Pak Hun were purged without mercy.

O Manlip was assigned to the team going to Chin'gol. He glanced around to see which of his neighbors would be joining him and recalled what Carpenter Kang had said a few days ago. On the day of the peasants' assembly in Sunch'ŏn, the village representatives had been given meal tickets. The party had run short of white paper, so some tickets were white and others blue. When a prankster quipped that the people with white tickets would be given dry fields while those with blue tickets would be assigned paddy land, the holders of the white tickets jumped to their feet in protest.

O Manlip was determined not to embarrass himself by making any hasty protests, even if they did hand out land that day. Still, he couldn't help feeling a certain apprehension. What if his neighbors took all the good land while he was up in Chin'gol? If they were handing out land for free, he had a right to his fair share. Just let someone get in his way. I'll smash in his skull without blinking an eye! Manlip decided, squeezing the handle of his rake.

The young man in the dog-fur coat hadn't even finished reading the verdict of the people's tribunal when a look of dread settled on Pak Yongje's face. He had heard that not all landlords were purged and had hoped that he would be among those allowed to stay.

He surveyed the crowd gathered at his front gate. There were some familiar faces: Tosŏp, his brother's estate agent for over two decades, Carpenter Kang, Kim Pokdong, young Kapsŏng, and Son Yongp'al. His eyes lingered on Son, who lived right next door.

He had heard of landlords spared on a few good words from their tenants. During the final days of colonial rule when grain quotas were high, Yongje had saved Son's family from starvation by giving them millet and sorghum. If only Son would tell the others of his generosity, Yongje thought.

He tried to catch his neighbor's eye, but Son simply shifted his sickle from one shoulder to the other and never turned to look in Yongje's direction. Yongje couldn't tell whether he was doing it on purpose or not.

"Give me all the keys," the young man demanded as he turned to Yongje.

Despair spread across the landlord's face. He pressed his eyelids closed for a moment, then opened them. A final gleam of hope suddenly flickered in his eyes.

He went into the main room. His son Hyŏk was peering through a crack in the door, an eight-inch dagger in his hand. Hyŏk's mother trembled fearfully as she clung to her son's arm. Yongje spread his arms to block Hyŏk, took the dagger away, and gave his son a scowl of caution. When he reappeared with his land deeds, the courtyard was full of peasants.

"These are the deeds for all my land. I'll give you everything. I only ask . . ."

"You aren't giving us anything. We're taking back what's rightfully ours."

"Fine. But I have something to ask in return."

The young man felt like yelling this was no time for idle talk, but he refrained. After all, he was responsible for taking this landlord to the town people's committee headquarters, and he hoped to avoid unnecessary problems. Better to humor the old fellow, he thought. Creativity! Yes, he must be creative in all matters.

"It's the reservoir."

"What about the reservoir?"

"Let me keep it."

A sarcastic grin spread across the young man's face. These landlords' lust for land is unbelievable! Encouraged by the young man's silence, Yongje went on to explain.

"A little while ago you said that I exploited the blood and sweat of the local people for that reservoir. But that's not true. They thought themselves lucky to work on the reservoir. It was better than being sent to work on the irrigation project in Anju or the repair works in Pyongyang. Just ask them! They'll tell you."

The old man scanned the crowd for someone to corroborate what he had said. His eyes met Tosŏp's.

"Oh, Tosŏp was there! He was in charge of mobilizing the workers. Tosŏp, why don't you tell this young gentleman what it was like?"

Tosŏp twitched his eyebrows. "I was just running errands

for him for free because he was my landlord's uncle," he said, then turned away.

Yongje realized that he was all alone. Now his only recourse was to plead with the young man. "Please believe me. I did nothing to be ashamed of."

The young man turned his eyes on Yongje, as if to ask, Is that why you're asking for the reservoir?

"I can finish it this spring. Please let me keep it."

"Look, old man. We forgive landlords who cooperate with our democratic reforms, but you have to forsake your landlord's mentality if you want to survive."

"Landlord's mentality?"

"Yes! I mean your insatiable greed for land!"

"But I'm not asking for the reservoir out of a greed for land."

"Then what is it?"

"I'm willing to give up my legal title to the reservoir. I simply want you to let me finish work on it!"

"What are you? A civil engineer?"

"Not really, but I'd like to finish it with my own hands."

Yongje didn't understand it himself. Why did he cling to the reservoir when he was willing to part with all his other property? Twenty years earlier he had been as devoted to the orchard as he was to the reservoir now. He spent nearly all his time there, but when the trees began to bear fruit, he lost interest. He didn't care that the trees had grown blighted and barren.

Later he had developed a consuming interest in forestry. Forests seemed the most wonderful thing in the world. They didn't require fertilizing or weeding. And they weren't affected by droughts and floods either. You had only to let them be, and they grew! If someone put a piece of forest land up for sale, Yongje bought it without a second thought. In those days his greatest pleasure was roaming his forest land on horseback.

Then, two years before liberation, he threw himself into the reservoir project. It cost him his longstanding friendship with Yun Kip'ung but he pushed ahead anyway. He wasn't motivated by the thought of pecuniary gain alone. It was as if he were driven by some force hidden inside him. No sooner had he begun the project than he was galloping to the site every day at dawn, not to return home until nightfall. His devotion to the project continued after liberation. Old Yongje's been bitten by the bug again, the villagers whispered.

"The ground has thawed, so we can begin working soon. It'll just take one more year to finish." His eyes shone with a strange gleam.

The young man thought that Yongje's request was nothing more than a ruse to hold on to his land until the reactionaries made a comeback. Typical landlord mentality! he fumed, but then he remembered that he was responsible for taking Yongje to the town people's committee headquarters. "We can discuss that when we get to party headquarters. Give me the keys."

This is hardly a matter for this young fellow to decide on his own, Yongje thought. "All right," he said. "I'll go get the keys, but I hope you'll put in a good word for me."

In the room his wife was still shaking like a leaf, her face pale with fear.

"I have to go into town," he said. Then he turned to his son. "Don't do anything rash. Just stay with your mother."

Hyŏk thought he saw a glimmer of hope in his father's face.

Yongje handed the string of keys to the young man and said, "Let me fetch my coat."

"That won't be necessary. You'll be right back," the young man replied as he gave the keys to Comrade Chang.

Chang waited for Yongje and the young man to step out the front gate, then went into the main room and began putting red seals on the furniture. Hyŏk glared at him as he helped his mother to the men's quarters. The old woman trembled so violently she couldn't get her shoes on. Hyŏk helped her put them on, then straightening up, he felt for the dagger he had hidden in his shirt. It was still there.

Outside, the villagers collected the tools that had been lying about the house and the utensils from the kitchen and put them in the barn. Kapsŏng discovered an insecticide sprayer in a corner of the barn and tried pumping it. A rusty screech pierced the air.

Carpenter Kang found some carpentry tools on a shelf in the barn. He glanced around quickly. There was no one in sight. He grabbed a wood plane and stuck it in his waistband. As he stepped out the back door of the kitchen, Son Yongp'al noticed a shovel and a hoe leaning against the rear wall. He looked to see if anyone was watching, then picked up the shovel and tossed it over the stone wall dividing the landlord's house from his. The shovel landed with a metallic thud. Too bad the old lady isn't over there to take these, he thought as he flung the hoe over the wall.

Someone was coming. It was Kim Pokdong. He was grinning from ear to ear, exposing two rows of yellowed teeth. Yongp'al's heart jumped. He'd been found out. He'd have to give Pokdong one of the tools to keep his mouth shut.

But just as Yongp'al was about to approach his neighbor to discuss the tools, he heard someone coming. They'd have to confer later, when they were alone.

Which one should I give him? Yongp'al wondered. I

need both. Why does the wretch have to show up now? Isn't there some way I could keep both? No . . . Look at that smirk. I'd never get away with it. I'll have to give him one of them. Well, it will have to be the hoe. On a farm a shovel's a lot more useful than a hoe.

Pokdong was headed for the barn with a winnower he had found under the eaves of the servants' quarters. I'll talk to him now, Yongp'al thought, but just as he was about to broach the subject, he noticed something poking from the waistband of Pokdong's pants. It was the tip of a woman's rubber shoe. Yongp'al stepped up to Pokdong and shoved the rubber shoe back inside his pants. His toothy smile was even broader than Pokdong's. There was no need to give up the shovel or the hoe now.

When he returned from the people's committee head-quarters, the young man in the dog-fur coat found Comrade Chang coming out of Hyŏk's room with a box-like object.

"What's that, comrade?" he asked.

"It's a radio. I found it in the closet," Chang replied.

"A radio?" The young man's eyes flashed. "Where is the student?"

Chang pointed to the men's quarters. The young man hurried to the entrance of the building and called, "Comrade student, could I see you for a minute?"

Hyŏk emerged, his eyes bloodshot.

"What's this?"

"It's a radio, as you can see."

"Yes, I know. But why do you have such a thing at home?"

Hyŏk stared at him in amazement.

"I know," cried the young man in the dog-fur coat. "You've been listening to the southern reactionaries' broadcasts on this thing, haven't you?"

"You can't hear anything on that radio."

"Why not?"

"It's not finished yet."

"Ah, so you were building it!" The young man's face relaxed, taking on a friendly air. "I heard you went to a technical high school. That's very good. Study hard and become a real scientist. We don't punish sons for their fathers' crimes. Our nation needs scientists. As you know, we're behind in science and technology. We need scientists to overcome our backwardness and become a truly advanced country like the Soviet Union!"

"What did you do with my father?"

"Oh, we had a few things to ask him so we took him to the people's committee headquarters in town. He'll be back soon."

The young man stepped through the gate, removed the nameplate, and hung a signboard in its place. It said "Village People's Committee Headquarters."

The crowd marched past the crossroads with the marble monument and headed for Hun's house. They walked with confidence now, the blades of their plowshares flashing ominously in the sun.

Tosŏp's dog Spotty began to bark. As the crowd approached, he scurried backward, still barking furiously, and when they stopped in front of Hun's house, he positioned himself at a stone's throw away and continued to bark.

Hun saw someone enter his house. Though he was standing at some distance, he could tell it was Tosŏp. Soon Tosŏp returned and whispered something to the young man in the dog-fur coat. A murmur swept through the crowd. Apparently, Tosŏp had told them that Hun was not in.

Hun stood up. He had been sitting on the slope by the

orchard, waiting for this moment. He heard a dog barking
as he headed down the hill. It had been barking for some
time, but somehow he felt as if the barking was coming
from inside his head now. Then it seemed as if it were
coming from far away, from a long-forgotten dream. He
tried to recall when he had heard the sound before. Then he
remembered. It was in the middle of the night. He had just
awakened from a terrible dream. A dog was barking in the
distance. Frightened, he burrowed into his mother's arms.
What a warm and cozy haven! He wasn't afraid anymore.

Mother! Oh, Mother! Hun thought as he approached the
house. His knees were shaking with fright.

The crowd turned to look at Hun. Their tanned faces
seemed to merge in a jumble. They parted to make way for
him. Yellow circles seemed to float in the path before him.

He went into the house and brought out the suitcase he
had packed earlier. His heart throbbed in his throat as he
bent to tie his shoes. The calm that he had felt as he stood
before his parents' grave deserted him now.

Suddenly he recalled that his father had died of a heart
attack. And his mother had died because her heart could not
withstand the fever. The doctor had said his heart was ex-
cellent, though. The world seemed to swim before him, but
the doctor had told him his heart was fine. He smiled despite himself. What shall be, shall be, he thought. Only then
did he recover some sense of calm.

Hun stepped out the gate, and the throng parted once
more. He could distinguish one face from the other now. He
recognized Tosŏp's shaven head and the ax hoisted on his
shoulder. And he could tell that the barking dog was
Tosŏp's Spotty.

"Wait a minute!" a voice commanded when he was a few
paces from the gate. It was the young man in the dog-fur

coat. "Come back and stand here!" he shouted, pointing to the gate.

Now I need permission to leave my own house, Hun realized.

The young man unfolded the paper he was holding and read aloud. "Resolution! The peasants' assembly hereby notifies the reactionary landlord Pak Hun of the following . . ." The young man looked up from the paper, apparently irritated by the dog's barking.

Tosŏp pushed through the crowd and threw a stone at Spotty, but the dog simply scampered out of range and kept on barking. I'll have to take him home, thought Tosŏp as he beckoned to the animal. The dog ignored his owner and continued to bark. Someone in the crowd told Tosŏp to put down the ax. The dog came to him when he did.

He grabbed the dog. "Shut up, you miserable mutt, or I'll kill you!" He then strode to his house, jerked the kitchen door open and flung the dog on the floor. In the room his wife had buried herself under a quilt and was trembling with fear. She had seen Tosŏp coming when she peeked outside to see why the dog was barking.

After Tosŏp banged the kitchen door shut and disappeared, the woman rubbed her palms together and prayed, "Please don't let anyone get hurt. Please don't let anything happen."

The young man began to read from the sheet of paper again: "The reactionary landlord Pak Hun spends his days drinking and criticizing the democratic revolution. He is also responsible for luring ignorant young men into a reactionary band and inciting them to murder the chairman of the town peasant committee. Moreover . . ." A gasp of surprise rose from the crowd and the young man stopped.

Ojaknyŏ had staggered from the house and was standing

at the gate, clinging to the gatepost. Her disheveled hair was tied back with a string, but her face was unwashed and still bore the ravages of fever. Only her eyes seemed alive with a luminous intensity.

Confident that Ojaknyŏ's appearance would serve his cause, the young man read on: "Moreover, he has used his power as landlord to seduce the daughter of one of his tenants, a married woman at that. Given these facts . . ."

"Wait!" Ojaknyŏ shouted. "Who wrote that nonsense?"

The young man looked up at her with surprise. "It's the resolution of the peasants' assembly," he answered in a kindly tone.

"Why did you write such lies?"

A look of astonishment and indignation flashed across his face. "Comrade, be careful what you say. We are trying to liberate you from the clutches of your reactionary landlord."

"I don't need to be liberated. Go back to your homes! All of you!"

"Has this slut gone clean out of her mind? The fever must have gotten to you," Tosŏp snarled, then rushed to the young man. "Comrade, please forgive her. She's been ill with typhoid fever. She's lost her senses." Then he glared back at his daughter. "Why don't you go back to bed, you miserable slut?"

"I'm not your daughter anymore."

"I'm going to rip your tongue out!" Tosŏp hollered as he lunged at her. The young man stuck out his arm to stop him.

"Calm down, comrade. This is no time for a family quarrel." Then, turning a stern face to Ojaknyŏ, he said, "We're too busy to argue with you."

He surveyed the crowd of bewildered faces and went on:

"Well then, let us continue. In view of these facts the peasants' assembly has determined that Pak Hun is an evil reactionary landlord and has unanimously agreed that all his property should be confiscated." He turned to Hun and said, "Hand over your keys."

Hun looked at Ojaknyŏ. She was in charge of all the household keys. He hoped she would surrender them and get it over with as soon as possible. But Ojaknyŏ staggered forward and placed herself between Hun and the young man, as if to shield Hun. "Why do you want the keys to someone else's property?"

Sparks flew from the young man's eyes. "Comrade, do you realize you could be punished for interfering with our operations?"

"This is my house! Nobody's going to lay a hand on it as long as I'm alive!"

The young man nodded understandingly. "You've been a servant in this house for a long time. I will report your case to party headquarters. They'll see that you get proper compensation. Have you been paid for your work here?"

"You don't understand!" Ojaknyŏ said.

The young man looked past her at Hun. "Did you pay her the wages you owe?"

But Ojaknyŏ answered before Hun had a chance to say anything. "He doesn't need to pay me."

"Well then, comrade," the young man replied in a soothing tone. "Just leave everything to us."

"No! No one's laying a finger on anything in this house!"

The young man pitied her. Imagine what she must have gone through. "Comrade, I told you. We understand how you've suffered, but we have to carry out these resolutions today."

"You don't understand anything."

"What don't we understand?"

"You don't understand anything!" Ojaknyŏ bit her lip. "We're married," she said, then closed her eyes gently. She seemed exhausted by the exertion.

The crowd began to whisper. Even the young man seemed surprised. Had things gone that far? In Pakch'ŏn, a female landowner had married a hired hand and been spared from the purge.

The young man searched the crowd for Ojaknyŏ's husband. The legal husband would have a decisive role to play in this. Ch'oe was standing at the back of the crowd. His face was flushed with anger and shame. He had come to the peasants' assembly after receiving a message from the town people's committee ordering him to testify in the land reform hearings. Ch'oe sensed the young man's eyes and blushed to the roots of his hair. "I have a question for Ojaknyŏ!" he shouted.

Ojaknyŏ shuddered and turned in the direction of the voice.

"Was there another man in your heart before you married me?"

Ojaknyŏ gazed blankly in her husband's direction. She didn't seem to understand the question at first. Then her eyes lit up again. They seemed to be saying that she was ready to contend with any accusations her husband might make.

"I'm asking if you loved Pak before you married me!"

Ojaknyŏ nodded and closed her eyes again.

"Well, I haven't thought of you as my wife for a long time, either!"

Ojaknyŏ seemed unable to stand any longer. She heaved a great sigh and collapsed at Hun's feet, the shadow of a smile playing on her pallid lips.

It's not true. It's all a misunderstanding. Hun kept shouting in his heart.

The young man whispered something to one of his colleagues. He was asking him to report this unexpected development to the comrade from provincial headquarters and ask for his advice. He didn't want to be accused of a lack of creativity again.

When he heard the report, the man from provincial headquarters smiled. "Well, that's quite interesting. If you want to catch a big fish, you need good hooks and bait. Let this Pak fellow go for now and keep a close watch on him."

And as the messenger turned to go, the man called out, "And comrade, get a photograph of Pak."

Tosŏp was furious. Imagine his own daughter spoiling everything! Why couldn't that whore just drop dead when she got that fever? Is she trying to ruin me? Does she want to see me purged?

He flung his ax onto the dirt floor between the rooms and stepped into the main room. "You idiot!" he bellowed at the sight of his wife trembling under the quilt. "How could you give birth to such a whore? You never should have taken her back after her husband dumped her. Do you want to see me ruined? Well, watch out! 'Cause if I fall, you can be sure you won't die peacefully in your bed either!"

His wife dared not respond. Only the quilt trembled as if it had a life of its own.

Tosŏp was too upset to sit at home. He grabbed his pipe and went outside. After hacking up a wad of phlegm, he stepped out the gate and glanced in the direction of the crossroads where the monument stood. Spurred by an idea, he returned to the house to get his ax. His large mouth was clamped shut with determination.

O Manlip's daughter, T'anshil, was drawing water from the well opposite the monument when she saw Tosŏp striding down the road with his ax. Though her pail was only half-filled, she hurried into the house.

Tosŏp stopped in front of the monument and faced it head-on. He had supervised construction of the monument commemorating Hun's grandfather's contributions to the community. He had set the foundation. He had poured the concrete. He had often stood like this to see that it was constructed properly. But this time was different. He was trying to figure out how to knock it down in a single stroke.

Tosŏp's breathing grew uneven. His eyebrows twitched several times. Finally, he swung his ax with a grunt. The monument cracked at the waist, and the upper part tumbled to the ground, sending an echo up and down the road.

Tosŏp swung the ax again. Then again, and again. "I'm going to kill you all! All of you!" he raged. Each time the ax fell, a new cloud of stone dust flew and another piece of the monument tumbled to the ground.

Kim Pokdong's wife peered out at the noise. "Look, Tosŏp's knocking down the monument," she cried. Pokdong, who was sitting in the corner smoking his pipe, looked over her shoulder. He didn't seem particularly surprised. He had witnessed far stranger, far more horrible things that day. "Don't go out today," his wife whispered nervously.

After knocking the monument to pieces, Tosŏp proceeded to hack apart the top section which had fallen at the first stroke. He was a man possessed. When he finished that task, he ran his red-rimmed eyes over the surrounding houses and shouted toward Hun's house, "To kill a serpent you have to smash its head!"

The words echoed through the village, then silence fell.

Pokdong's wife peeked outside. "I think he's gone," she said. "Why don't you go out and see if we could use a piece of the monument for a fulling stone?"

She had gotten the idea watching Tosŏp smash the monument. Whenever she had clothes to full, she always had to go to Grandma Bullye's. It was extremely inconvenient. This was a perfect chance to get her own fulling stone. The monument stone was smooth as silk. A piece of it would be a perfect fulling stone if her husband could find a big enough piece.

Pokdong sat puffing on his pipe. He felt bad enough about the rubber shoes he had filched from Old Yongje's place. "You'd better hurry, dear, before someone else gets them," his wife urged. She had already forgotten that she had just told him to stay home that day.

Pokdong puffed on his pipe in silence. Then he had a thought. Those stones aren't the same as shoes. They aren't part of the monument anymore. They're just rocks lying on the ground. No different from any other rock. It's no crime to pick up a stone.

Pokdong rose and went outside. He picked up the biggest piece of stone, but it was too heavily inscribed to make a good fulling block. He picked up a smoother stone, but it was too small. Why couldn't Tosŏp hack them into more usable pieces?

Kapsŏng came out and began to sift through the rubble. He turned over the large stone that Pokdong had looked at earlier. "Hey, I already got that one," Pokdong called out. I'll use that one for a stoop, he thought. And as long as I'm at it, I'll get a whetstone too.

O Manlip's wife stepped outside. She was annoyed with her husband for missing this opportunity. Everyone else was back already. Why had he allowed himself to get dragged off to Chin'gol? The fool! He could be getting us a couple of cornerstones for that stupid shed he's always worrying about! She called to her daughter in the house. "T'anshil, come out here!"

Little Tangson unbolted the plank gate and stepped out. His grandfather had returned home early, before the people's assembly had finished, bolted the gate, and remained inside. Tangson picked up one of the stone fragments and took it to his grandfather, but Old Ko hurled it over the hedge when he saw it.

Yun Kip'ung felt as if he were going mad. He may have been wrong to expect his former tenants to speak up for him, but how could Song Kwanho just stand there, blinking like a fool, when they had clearly made an agreement?

"Kwanho," he called out, unable to control his indignation any longer. "Why don't you tell them? Remember? For the last year I've been tilling the 2,000 thousand *p'yŏng* you used to work."

Kwanho lowered his eyes. "I can't say what never happened."

The blood drained from the tip of Squire Yun's pockmarked nose.

"What do you mean, never happened?"

"I can't do it, even if it means giving up the ox and cart." Of course it wasn't that Kwanho didn't yearn for the ox and cart. But something even more important was at stake. If he wasn't careful, he could lose the land he had been working!

Earlier, on the way back from the peasants' assembly, Comrade Shin had whispered something in his ear. If he said anything to defend or aid the reactionary absentee landlord Yun Kip'ung, he might as well give up living in that village. Kwanho stole a glance at Shin. He could tell

Shin wasn't going to listen to any excuses later. What could he do? He had no place to go. He had to give up the oxcart. The broad rump of the ox rose before his eyes, then disappeared again. If only there was a way!

Squire Yun was desperate. He had to secure enough land to feed his family, even if he had to cultivate it himself. Besides, he had to hold on to some land, however small a plot, so he could recover his property when things changed again. But his plans were ruined by that treacherous tenant.

Yun glared at Kwanho's dirty face. Why, that very morning Song had assured him there was nothing to worry about! They're all a bunch of ignoramuses. That's why they live that way, Yun muttered to himself.

Two of his former tenants stepped forward. The elder of the two glanced at Comrade Shin, then turned to address Yun. "You know that paddy land you sold us? We want our money back."

Yun had been trying to sell off some of his land ever since he heard of the impending land reform. He offered the land at dirt-cheap prices and even went so far as to spread a rumor that this may be the last chance to buy land before transactions were forbidden. Yun had kept this scheme from Hun for fear the other landlords would put their land up for sale, bringing prices down and making prospective buyers suspicious. He had told Hun of his ploy to make it look like he was tilling a piece of the land himself, because the landowners' position would be strengthened if more of them remained in the area.

Squire Yun's plan was not as successful as he had hoped, however. The peasants simply didn't have the money to buy the land, no matter how low the price. The two men standing before him were the best off of his tenants. Pang Handol had been raising a calf for the last year, and Ch'ŏn

Ondal had a large sow. By selling the animals and their chickens, they hoped to collect enough money to make the initial payments. Of course, that didn't cover the full cost of the land, but Yun had kindly offered to accept the rest in grain over the coming years.

And so the transactions were made. For days afterward, the two farmers gloated in private, but now they realized their mistake. The new authorities were going to seize all land and redistribute it, theirs included.

Handol thought he should be the one to speak up, seeing he was older and more articulate than his friend. "Here's the contract. Now give us back our money."

Yun's lips twitched as he spoke. "What's this? Some kind of game? You begged me to sell them to you, and now . . . "

"Things are different now. Hurry up and give us back our money!"

The crowd held their breath as they watched the drama. They felt lucky not having bought any land, though it had been for lack of money.

Squire Yun went inside. He had been living in a room at Kwanho's house ever since he returned to the village. Removing his felt hat from a hook on the wall, he returned with two pieces of paper hidden in the crown.

"Here, I'll write off the rest of your payments, if you insist," he said as he handed the men their promissory notes for the rest of the payment in grain.

Comrade Shin snatched the pieces of paper and tore them to bits. Drawing courage from that, Ch'ŏn Ondal, the younger farmer, stuttered, "Gi-gi-give us ba-ba-back the mo-mo-money, ra-ra-right now!"

Beads of sweat gathered on Yun's pockmarked nose. However, he realized that in a dangerous situation like this he had to keep his wits about him. "I don't have the money with me," he replied firmly.

"What?"

"I already sent it to Pyongyang."

"When?"

"My wife took it with her the last time she visited."

Handol's face paled at the news, but Ondal blinked in surprise. "No, we pa-pa-paid you a-a-after she lel-left," he said.

"Right!" Handol exclaimed. "I saw your wife getting on the train to Pyongyang with a sack of grain when I was coming back from selling my calf."

"No, no, you're wrong. She came after you paid me!"

Handol's eyes flashed. "Let me see your money belt," he demanded and flung his spade aside. Everybody knew Yun carried his money belt inside the waistband of his pants.

"Are you crazy?" Yun shouted as he took a step backward.

Handol grabbed Yun's arm.

"What do you think you're doing?"

Then Ondal grabbed the other arm.

"How dare you?" Yun yelled with all the authority he could muster. The two men hesitated for an instant. What were they doing, laying hands on their former landlord? They had never dreamed of doing such a thing before. But what did that matter now? They simply had to get their money back. The two men fumbled at Yun's waistband.

"You thieves! Hey, isn't somebody going to arrest these crooks?" Yun squirmed and looked around the crowd in desperation. But no one came to his aid. If he wanted to get out of this predicament, he would have to do it on his own.

"Take your hands off me, you thieves. Let's talk. It may

be a lawless world but you can't commit robbery in broad daylight!" he pleaded, but the two men kept fumbling at his pants.

All of a sudden Yun noticed the stake used for tying the ox. He hurled himself sideways, knocking his head against the stake. "Help me, help me! I'm dying!" he screamed. Blood began pouring from the top of his head. The two farmers stared at him in bewilderment. Yun wrapped his hands around his head and screamed, "Help me, help me! I'm dying! I'm dying!"

The two farmers' eyes flashed at the sight of Yun's money belt which was exposed when he raised his hands. They swooped down and began untying it. Yun bolted upright and grabbed hold of the money belt, but the two men twisted his wrists to loosen his grip. His fingers left bloody marks on the white cloth. No sooner had they untied the belt than the two men disappeared around the corner of the house.

"Someone nab those murderous thieves!" Yun shrieked, but no one moved.

A strange feeling swept over O Manlip as he watched Yun's ordeal. Is this really happening? he wondered. The world *has* turned upside down! I guess that's why people say you can't tell about a man until he's dead and buried. I surely haven't seen anything like this before!

Comrade Shin muttered to himself as he rolled a cigarette. Well, I've done my job today. It's not my fault you're bleeding. You can bleed to death for all I care.

Squire Yun rose, grasping his head with one hand. He went inside and returned with his hat and coat. Then he climbed into the oxcart standing in the corner of the yard and turned his bloodshot eyes to Kwanho. He was going to ask him to drive him to Sunan, or at least as far as Dr. Kim's in Karakkol.

Kwanho glanced at Comrade Shin, then turned away, noisily blowing the snot from his nose.

Yun climbed down from the cart. His heart burned at Kwanho's betrayal. "I've been bitten by my own dog," he muttered as he walked away from the village. "Yeah, I've been bitten by my own dog."

As Yun came to the crossroads, he stumbled on a stone lying in front of Old Ko's house. It was a piece of the monument that he had helped to build. Yun didn't even notice what it was, though. All he did was grumble: "Why's this damned stone lying in the middle of the road?"

He stopped in front of Dr. Kim's clinic. The door was locked. He knocked, and a shadow flitted across the windowpane. It was Dr. Kim. The door didn't open, though.

"It's me. Yun from Chin'gol," he said.

"We're closed today," snapped a voice from inside.

"I just need to have my wound dressed," Yun countered.

But there was no answer.

Oh, yeah? I heard you refused poor patients, and now you're treating me like a pauper. What's the world coming to? Squire Yun's squat frame wobbled perilously as he headed down the road to Sunan.

Hun was sitting beside the old tomb on the hill behind the village. He kept trying to figure out something, but it was all a muddle and a confusion. All he could do was repeat the word "misunderstanding" over and over again.

Hyŏk climbed the hill to join him. He was holding a piece of their grandfather's monument.

"How could those bastards do this?" he exclaimed, shaking the stone in Hun's face. "They've taken Father and I don't know what's happened to him. He said he'd be right back, but the people at party headquarters say they took him to Pyongyang for some kind of investigation."

Hun too was suspicious when he heard this.

"He didn't even take a coat. I know he's strong for his age, but he shouldn't be going around without a coat in this weather."

Hun took solace in the fact that they had taken him away in his shirtsleeves. They must plan to release him soon, he thought.

"I'm going to Pyongyang right now. And if they've harmed Father, I'm going to get those bastards!" Hyŏk clenched his teeth in anger as he shook the stone again. "Did you see this? Why did they have to destroy the monument? What wrong did it do?"

Suddenly Hun recalled his cousin's excitement the morning he brought news of Kwŏn's murder. At the time Hun had felt a certain anger tinged with sorrow. He had wanted to chide Hyŏk for getting so excited by the thought of bloodshed. But now he felt something quite different. He felt that it was his cousin who was bleeding, bleeding inside his own heart.

After Hyŏk left, Hun remained by the old tomb. His eyes kept returning to the fragment of stone from the monument. He felt as if he too was bleeding somewhere deep inside.

As evening approached, Hun returned home to find Ojaknyŏ, hair neatly combed, starting the fire in the kitchen.

"What are you doing? You should rest for a few more days."

"I'm all right now."

"No. What if you have a relapse? You should rest for a few more days."

"I'm better now."

After clearing away Hun's supper tray, Ojaknyŏ stepped quietly into his room.

"I think you'd better rest a few more days."

"I'm all right now, really. I've already put you to so much trouble . . . "

"Don't worry about that. Just rest a little longer."

"No, I'm really all right. People like me don't die so easily. . . . But sir . . . please forgive my impertinence of this afternoon."

"You shouldn't have exerted yourself so much . . . especially when you're so sick."

"I didn't mean to do it. It just . . . happened. And last night . . . Please forgive me." Ojaknyŏ's wan cheeks reddened as she lowered her head.

How could this meek-looking woman act so boldly? Hun wondered.

After a moment's silence, Ojaknyŏ took a bundle from the corner and pushed it across the floor to Hun. She must have put it there while he was out. "Please, sir, take these back." Hun looked down at the bundle. "It's the fabric your mother bought."

"But I gave it to you!" he protested. Suddenly he felt he had been wrong to stay. Too bad they hadn't driven him away after the peasants' assembly. "This house is yours now," he said.

"No! Please don't say such things! This house belongs to you, always." She turned her burning eyes on him.

"Don't get me wrong," he explained. "I've been thinking of giving you this house for some time. That is, if your husband doesn't object."

"Sir, please don't say such things." Her eyes grew moist and seemed to plead with him.

"But . . . " Hun paused when he realized he didn't mean what he was going to say. "Well, at least take the fabric."

"But your mother bought it for . . ."

"What does that matter? I won't be needing it."

Her tear-filled eyes searched his face, but then she became distracted. The call of a cuckoo was drifting on the evening breeze. Her eyes took on a dreamy cast. "It's the cuckoo from Maiden Rock," she murmured.

Hun had heard the legend of Maiden Rock when he was a child.

Long ago there was a rich man living in Karakkol. His house had twelve gates, like an enormous palace. The man had only one son, and this son fell in love with a servant girl. The young master was sent to Seoul to study. As he was leaving, he asked his sweetheart to wait for him. He did not return for many years, though, and the servant girl was afraid the young master had forgotten her. She thought it presumptuous to have hoped he would marry a wretched servant girl like herself. And so she married someone else. Her husband was a terrible ruffian. He beat her over the most trifling matters. Every night the girl climbed the mountain and prayed to the mountain gods, asking them to turn her into a rock. Then, one summer's night, thunder and lightning shook the heavens and the earth, and the maiden kneeling in prayer was turned into a rock. That winter the young master returned. When he heard what happened to his sweetheart, he ran up the hill, threw his arms around the rock and cried. It was mid-winter but the rock was as warm as human flesh. The young master cried for many days and finally died with the rock in his arms. The following spring, pink azaleas bloomed there, and deep in the woods a cuckoo sang a mournful song.

When Hun was a child, he had climbed the hill to pick azaleas at Maiden Rock. It really had looked like a young woman kneeling at the brink of the cliff. And a cuckoo was singing a mournful song then, too.

"Whenever I hear the cuckoo, I feel so lucky," Ojaknyŏ murmured. The dream-like gleam in her moist eyes grew stronger. "I have so much more than I deserve."

6

Several village women had gathered by the well at the crossroads.

"Ojaknyŏ used to be such a shy girl," said Kapsŏng's mother, the Widow Yi, as she sorted through the wild leeks she had come to wash.

"Shy? Why, she's sullen and stubborn as an ox," responded Kim Pokdong's wife. The woman had drawn her pail of water and was ready to hoist it onto the top of her head and carry it home. But she paused now, her headpad in place, and turned to the Widow Yi. "You know, the other day when she was sick, I went to look in on her. I asked if I could borrow a brass bowl, but she refused and made the biggest fuss."

"Well, you know what? That slut came to our house this morning and searched my kitchen!" O Manlip's wife exclaimed from her spot by the well. In fact, she had taken a sieve from Hun's kitchen when she went to his house pretending to check on the patient, and Ojaknyŏ had discovered it that very morning.

"Young folks just aren't what they used to be," the widow sighed, half to herself.

"You're right there! After all these years we still can't look our husbands in the face, but these young hussies . . . " Pokdong's wife pursed her lips in disapproval.

"Well, I couldn't do something like that, even if my life depended on it! Imagine! Getting up in front of all those people . . . and with her own husband looking on? Heaven help her! Of course, I guess they've been shacked up for a long time now," Manlip's wife added with a wrinkle of her nose.

"When a young man and a woman live under the same roof for three years, something's bound to happen," the Widow Yi muttered as she rinsed her leeks.

Manlip's wife gasped as if she had just remembered something. "You know what? People are saying she wasn't sick from the fever. Seems she had a bad case of morning sickness."

"You're kidding!" exclaimed the Widow Yi.

Manlip's wife was pleased with the sensation she had caused. "Oh, yes," she added. "This morning when she came to my house I could see she was carrying herself differently."

"Heaven forbid!"

Pokdong's wife removed her headpad and returned to squat beside the others. "I thought she might be pregnant last summer. I'd heard their well water was nice and cool so I went over to take a bath. Well, when she asked me to scrub her back, I could see her nipples were darker than before. Yes, I thought something was fishy."

"But isn't it strange the way her husband acted?" the Widow Yi wondered aloud. "I never would have pegged him for the type to give up his wife without a fight."

"Oh, he's got his reasons."

Like what? the Widow Yi seemed to ask as she stared gap-mouthed at Manlip's wife, a blackened tooth revealed between her lips.

Manlip's wife carefully set the dipper in her pail, prolonging the suspense. "They paid him off. I hear he got a load of jewelry and stuff. That Ch'oe always did have a nose for money."

The widow nodded as if to say that made sense. Pokdong's wife gazed at Manlip's wife, awed at her ability to keep up on the latest gossip. "So that's why he bought that chicken from me yesterday," she sighed. "He said he was having a drinking party today. Darn! If only I'd known! I'd have charged him more."

Hun was leafing through a pile of old newspapers when Samdŭk came to tell him somebody wanted to see him. Hun stepped outside to find Ojaknyŏ's husband. "How are you?" Ch'oe asked with a smile. "If you're not too busy, I'd like to invite you for a drink."

Noting Hun's hesitation, Ch'oe explained. "I meant to treat you the other day but you ended up paying. I'd like to return the favor."

For some reason, Hun felt like getting drunk with this fellow.

"Are you feeling all right?" Ch'oe asked. "You don't look well."

"Oh, I'm fine. I always look this way."

"I hope you don't think me rude for coming here like this. I don't know about you, but I can't drink without a drinking buddy."

"I often drink alone."

"Really? Then you're a true drinking man." Ch'oe smiled with a flash of white teeth. "So, have you heard the latest rumor?"

Hun turned to give Ch'oe a questioning look.

"I mean the rumor about me selling my wife. Hŭngsu says it's the talk of the village."

So he's come to ask for money, Hun thought. Offensive though it was, Hun decided to oblige the man as best he could.

"What's the matter? You look pale."

"Well, if that's what you came to talk about . . . " Hun saw no need to go all the way to the tavern to bargain over a figure.

"I realize you can't be too happy about such talk, either, but it's only natural that people should think that way. After all, men have been known to sell their wives."

Ch'oe sounded as if he hoped for a hefty payoff. He paused, as if to think, then continued. "You know, I met a fellow like that once myself. Back when I was foreman at the Hoech'ang Gold Mine. There was this barmaid. She was a pretty young thing . . . had this way of pouting and smiling and making eyes at you. I liked that. Well, I fell for her hook, line and sinker. Of course, this must sound awfully stupid to someone like you. I'll bet you've had some fine romances. But just listen to my story, all right?"

Ch'oe reeked of garlic and liquor. He said he had seen Hŭngsu. Perhaps they had shared a drink. Or was this fellow drunk from the day before?

"Anyway, this girl was married. Her husband was a real bum . . . lived off his wife's tips. And he got wind of her and me. So one night I find him waiting at the entrance of the mine after work. Well, one look and I knew we'd been found out. Of course, I always figured I'd have to deal with him sooner or later. Anyway, he told me to come with him. I followed him and we ended up in this deserted hollow way up in the mountains. Then he pulls out this kitchen knife and pokes it at my chest, and he says, 'You've been playing around with my wife, haven't you?' So I told him the truth. But you've got to understand something—it wasn't out of fear of that knife. Not at all. Why, knives are a part of life for folks like me. It's just that even a cardshark tells the truth about matters of that nature. Though it might cost him his life. You get my drift?" Ch'oe threw Hun a meaningful glance.

"Well, this guy was flabbergasted. I guess he never expected me to come right out with the truth. He just stood there, staring at me with this stunned look on his face. And then he takes the knife off me. After that, I figured he was going to give me his wife. And I was ready to take her. So I went back to my inn and waited, but she didn't show up. I couldn't wait any longer so I went to her house to see what was going on. I was almost there when someone jumps out and blocks my way. It was the husband. He said he was on his way to my place. He said he'd beaten his wife to make her confess, but she insisted there was nothing between her and me. I said she was probably afraid of what he might do. He said that couldn't be it because he'd told her he'd let her go live with her lover, but she kept insisting she didn't have one.

"Isn't that strange? All along she'd been pestering me to run off with her, and now she wouldn't go! So her husband and I decided to go have it out with her. Pretty low, eh?" Ch'oe smiled bitterly. "But I figured it was better to bring everything out in the open, instead of shilly-shallying around. Anyway, we confronted her, but she kept insisting that she'd had nothing to do with me. Well, I realized she'd lied to me and so I walked right out of their house. But you know what? Her husband followed me outside and said it was obvious that she'd been fooling around, no matter what she said. And then he asked me to take her. He said that he couldn't go on living with a whore and I could have her for twenty thousand *nyang*. At the time, I actually had the money because I'd been having good luck at the tables, but I wasn't going to pay a single penny for that deceitful bitch. I told him I wouldn't take her, even if he gave her to me for free. So then he says the least I could do was pay him for sleeping with her. It ended in a knife fight. This is my trophy."

Ch'oe lifted his sleeve to reveal the scar he had shown the tavern mistress a few days before. "But that's not all. Not long after that she came to see me at the inn. It was a moonlit night. I asked what she was doing there and she said I was a fool for telling her husband the truth. Then she said we should get together again, without her husband knowing. I was so mad I belted her without even thinking. She screamed and covered her face, but I could see her nose was bleeding. Still, I wasn't sorry. I told her I never wanted to see her again, and that was the end of it.

"What a pair! Have you ever heard of such a thing? If that bastard husband of hers wanted to live with the whore, he should have, and she should have made a choice—live with me openly or go back to her lousy husband. Unbelievable!"

Ch'oe turned his bloodshot eyes to Hun. "Compared with that whore, Ojaknyŏ's worth two million *nyang* for sure! She's mighty good-looking, wouldn't you say? And there aren't many women who can speak their minds in front of so many people like she did yesterday. As a matter of fact, after I spoke to you at the tavern the other day, I decided to take her back. I figured it was time to let bygones be bygones. I even rented a house in Sunan. But when I heard what she said yesterday, I changed my mind. Hŭngsu said I'd be a rich man if I took her back. He said I could have your house, too. But you know what? I may look like a bum, but I know how a real man should act. I'd never sell my honor for a house. But now people are saying I took money for my wife."

"I'm willing to do anything I can to help you."

"Help me?" Ch'oe's eyes sparkled. "What do you mean?"

"Please don't get me wrong. I want to be frank with you, too."

"Frank? About what? You mean you're offering me money? What do you take me for? You haven't understood a word I've said! What good is money, anyway? It comes and goes as it pleases. I can't say I've ever been rich, but I certainly haven't been a slave to money either. I've had my share of hard times but I've always managed to get along. And lately I've made a killing at the gambling tables."

Ch'oe pulled a fistful of red military scrips from his pocket and shoved them in Hun's face.

"I'm still gambling. It's an old habit I just can't shake. They offered to make me vice chairman of the youth committee in Sunan, and I accepted. These days a title like that can come in real handy, you know. It's a nice shield for a gambler. Anyway, don't talk to me about money. The world may be going to the dogs, but I'd never stoop to selling my wife. Understand?"

Hun felt he did understand why Ch'oe had come to see him. He wasn't asking for money. The man was in pain. He had lost his wife, and now people were saying he had sold her. Ch'oe had obviously hoped to vent his anger and pain, and Hun could understand how he felt.

Maybe I should try to make him understand that there really isn't anything going on between Ojaknyŏ and me? Hun thought. But it was useless. Ch'oe would never believe him. It was only natural. So he simply said, "People will talk until they get tired of talking."

"You're right there. But if anyone breathes a word of that trash to me, I'll tear his lousy tongue out."

Ch'oe's hand trembled as he pulled out a cigarette and lit it. Then he offered the pack to Hun.

"Thanks, but I don't smoke."

"Oh, I forgot," Ch'oe said and walked on in silence. His cigarette must have gone out for he paused to relight it. "Why is that brat following me all the time?" Ch'oe muttered as he looked into the distance.

Hun looked through the trees to see Samdŭk approaching with his A-frame carrier on his back.

"You know, the other day when you and I were drinking at the tavern, I saw him squatting out back when I went out to take a piss. I think he was eavesdropping on us. The boy's my brother-in-law, but I can't stand him. He never even says hello. Why, you'd think he was deaf and dumb! The other day, he saw me for the first time in years, but he didn't even nod. And just now, Tangson was too afraid to go get you, so I asked Samdŭk instead, and he walked away without a word. Only later did I realize he did go to your house. I know he's never been one for small talk, but the boy's downright rude! Brothers-in-law are usually so close, but he's never showed me the least bit of affection!"

Hun recalled what Ojaknyŏ had said when she had learned her brother had been following him: Samdŭk isn't that kind of boy. At the time, Hun had thought that Samdŭk would only get worse, and now it looked like he had taken over the spying mission from Tangson.

Ch'oe took a long draw on his cigarette. "Oh, I don't care. It's not like I'm looking to him for favors. Well, let's get going. I'm hungry and I'd sure like a drink. The chicken should be done by now. I bought one and asked the woman at the tavern to cook it for us."

And sure enough, blue smoke was rising from the chimney of the tavern next to the big chestnut tree. Ch'oe strode ahead, as if he could think of nothing but drinking now.

The next morning Hun woke with a pounding headache. He had drunk far too much the day before. Hun had wanted to get good and drunk so he had tossed down every drink Ch'oe had poured. Still, his hangover pained him less than the shame that lingered in his mind.

The drunker Hun got, the shabbier he felt in comparison to Ch'oe. He couldn't help feeling that Ch'oe was a man of grand proportions whom he could never hope to equal. Ch'oe's behavior toward the man he believed to be his wife's lover made Hun feel shabby and small. But then he felt a sudden twinge of rebellion. This misunderstanding must not go on. He had to make this man understand. "You've got it all wrong," he blurted out. "I'll give you my house. You can live there with Ojaknyŏ. I've never laid a hand on her."

Even as he spoke, Hun regretted his pettiness. But it was too late. Ch'oe's eyes blazed. "What do you take me for? Are you still babbling about your stupid purity? Poor Ojaknyŏ. *How did she ever get stuck with such a miserable weakling?*" Ch'oe hollered, whacking Hun across the cheek.

Hun's face stung and his head swam. Ch'oe sprang from the table, threw a handful of military scrips to the tavern mistress, then glared back at Hun. "I don't want to have anything to do with you again!" he shouted before striding out the door.

Hun's nose did not bleed, but his eyes watered from the pain. He pressed his hands over his eyes. He felt relieved somehow but at the same time ashamed of his smallness.

His shame was even greater now that he was sober. *Are you still babbling about your stupid purity? Poor Ojaknyŏ. How did she ever get stuck with such a miserable weakling?* Why, he was more despicable than the barmaid Ch'oe had met in that mining town! How come he couldn't confront his emotions honestly and make a definite choice?

Hun knew he was a coward. But he also knew he could be nothing else. He groaned in disgust.

Hun heard footsteps approaching, then the door slid open. It was Hyŏk.

"What's wrong? Are you sick?" he asked as he stepped into the room. He must have just returned from Pyongyang.

"Oh, it's just a headache . . . " Hun sat up and untied the towel he had wrapped around his pulsing temples. "Well, did you locate your father?"

"No. The people at provincial headquarters said they'd never heard of him. I traipsed all over town for three days but I didn't learn a thing."

"But the town committee said he'd been sent to provincial headquarters, didn't they?"

"Oh, yes. I stopped by the town committee on my way back from Pyongyang, but they said Father had definitely been sent to provincial headquarters. I told them I'd just been there, but they said all they knew was that he'd been sent to Pyongyang."

Hyŏk stared into space for a moment. "I don't believe them. They've sent him somewhere. I heard all kinds of horror stories when I was in Pyongyang. In some regions, landlords have been sent to the mountains to clear fields. In other places, they were simply driven off their lands. Some have been thrown out with only the shirts on their backs, while others have been allowed to take blankets and things. In some places, their belongings have been divided up on the spot, by lottery, but in other regions they've sealed the houses and carted off the furniture later, the way they did at our house. I'm afraid they've dragged Father off to some horrible place."

Hun wasn't so sure. He had read a newspaper editorial that called for the mobilization of former landlords in advanced industries, instead of leaving them dependent on the land. It may have been nothing more than propaganda, but Hun didn't see much point in sending an old man like his uncle to the mountains to do hard labor.

"Why didn't you stay in Pyongyang for a few days and make more inquiries?"

"Well, he clearly wasn't taken to provincial headquarters." Hyŏk paused, biting his lower lip. "I don't think he'll be coming back."

"Why don't you go to Saetgol and see what happened to Old Master Hong?" Hun suggested.

Hong was a wealthy landowner with large holdings along the border between P'yŏngwon and Taedong counties. He was sure to have been a primary target of the purge. If Hyŏk could find out what happened to him, he might be able to figure out what they had done with the other landlords.

"That's an idea. I'll go and see what became of him . . . Oh, it looks like rain." Hyŏk rose to leave, then paused to search his pockets. "By the way, did you read that article?"

Hun used to get the newspapers from his neighbors when they went to Pyongyang or Sunan, but he hadn't seen one lately. He gave his cousin a curious look.

"I had one, but I must have lost it," Hyŏk said. "The *Workers' Daily* had an article on you."

"On me?"

"It said a progressive landlord-intellectual had married the daughter of one of his tenants."

Hun felt the blood pulsing in his temples. Two days earlier Hŭngsu had come asking for a photograph. When he said he had none, Hŭngsu had pleaded, saying it was for a good cause. But Hun really didn't have any photographs. He never had liked being photographed and had been careless with the photographs he had taken. Hŭngsu begged. A group photo would do, he said. Hun replied that the only photograph he had was one taken on his first birthday. Hŭngsu had left, disgruntled and empty-handed.

As a result, the article had come out without a picture. But that was small consolation. The fact that an article like that had been published at all made Hun's face burn. Hun let out another groan.

There was a second landlord purge. The man who had bought Yun Kip'ung's house in Chin'gol was targeted. He had moved to the country because his consumptive son needed clean air and quiet. The man raised some chickens and a few goats. He didn't have much land, but he was purged for being a man of leisure.

Myŏnggu's father, who lived in Chestnut Hollow, was purged too. In the first purge, they had seized the land he rented out to sharecroppers, but he had been allowed to keep the land he tilled himself, despite his son's reactionary crime, on the principle that a man should not be punished for the crimes of his son or father. However, this time the rest of his land was confiscated, apparently because he had hired peasants to till it. People said that he had actually been purged in retaliation for his son's murder of Kwŏn, chairman of the local peasants' committee.

Grandma Bullye's land was seized as well. The old woman was over seventy and had worked hard all her life, finally buying a small patch of land with the money she had accumulated from odd jobs and cotton weaving. During the final years of colonial rule, she was frequently summoned to the police station for failing to meet the grain quota and hiding barley under her stone floor or stuffing her pillow with rice. And she had often been marched through the village carrying her loom on her back as punishment for weaving cloth instead of the straw ropes and sacks the colonial authorities demanded.

Grandma Bullye was found dead the day after the second purge. She had hanged herself from a beam in her house.

"She did the right thing," Old Ko muttered as he sat among the neighbors who had gathered after her death. "What's there to live for? Nothing but trouble these days."

"You'd better watch your tongue, old man," snapped Tosŏp.

Old Ko turned his grizzled face to Tosŏp. "What, have I said something wrong?"

"Why don't you just keep quiet? The old woman was senile. Don't you see? That's why she hanged herself."

"So how'd she go senile overnight?"

"Listen, old man. I know it's too bad the old woman got caught in the purge, but on the other hand when you're trying to accomplish something really big, you can't always be thinking of all the little things. It's just like the irrigation project. Remember? The people who owned land where the dam and feeder lines were going to be dug were mad as hell. But when you think about it now, you can see that the loss of that land is nothing compared with the huge area the dam made fit for farming. I'll bet hardly anyone's against the dam now. It's the same thing with Grandma Bullye. There are bound to be a few problems when you're trying to accomplish something as big as this."

"You sure have picked up a lot of high-faluting words lately. That all sounds very grand, but words can't solve everything. Take the dam for example. It's lucky it turned out all right. But what if it hadn't? A lot of people would be hurting now. And just think! No one hanged himself because of the dam."

"So you don't think land reform will work?"

"I don't know. We'll just have to wait and see. But I don't like what I've seen lately."

"If you don't know what's going on, why don't you just keep your mouth shut?"

"I didn't want to say anything. You goaded me into it."

"Well, what did the landlord ever do for you?"

"You've done better by the landlord than me!"

"Huh? What's gotten into this old loon?"

"Is that any way to talk to an old man?"

"I know what you're trying to do." Tosŏp shook his pipe at the old man. "Yes, I know. You're in cahoots with the reactionary landlords. But it's too late! There's nothing you can do."

"Ha! Are you trying to scare me? Well, do what you like. I haven't much longer to live. What do I have to look forward to? You've got plenty of time left, so I wish you a long and prosperous life!"

"Damned fool!" Tosŏp sputtered and turned to leave. "There's no helping the ignorant old loon. He still doesn't know which way the world is turning. But he'll find out soon enough."

As he trudged up the hill to his house, Tosŏp coughed up several wads of phlegm. Then suddenly he felt a kind of mist settling before his eyes. He looked into the sky to see if it was clouding over. A layer of mist seemed to be hanging in the overcast sky. He blinked, but the mist didn't disappear. He rubbed his eyes with the back of his hands. The mist lingered in front of him still. I'm getting old, he thought. I'm old, just like old Grandma Bullye.

Suddenly he wondered if the old woman hadn't been

right to kill herself. But the next moment he chided himself for his weakness. I can't give up! I have to get through this. He clenched his fists, but his square jaw trembled ever so slightly.

It never did rain. The clouds lifted and the sky cleared. Just as the frozen earth thawed, the sky too seemed to be stepping slowly toward spring. Hun was sitting by the old tomb, contemplating some new pasqueflower shoots, when he saw his cousin climbing toward him.

"I think something dreadful has happened to Father. He must've been sent to a labor camp or killed. Otherwise, we'd have some news of him by now. We were fools to stay on until they implemented the land reform. Old Master Hong moved his whole family to Pyongyang long ago. He was smart. You and I may have been spared in the first purge but that doesn't mean we're safe. There's already been a second one. They didn't want to frighten people too much, so they began the purge in the backward villages and spared most of the smaller landowners, but just wait!

"God only knows when they'll feed me to the vultures. They let me off the other day because I am an engineering student, but how long will that last? And they'll get you too. Class background is everything to them. There's no escape if you're the son of a landlord. It's just a matter of time. That's why I've decided to go South."

Hyŏk stared at Hun as if to ask what he meant to do. "You know, I went to see a classmate of mine in Pyongyang. He said that the communists are making some kind of borderline at the thirty-eighth parallel so we can't just sit around waiting for the country to be unified. He also said they have a strong organization. They're not likely to collapse soon. The only way to break them is to attack from outside. He said he's going to the South, since our school's in Seoul, and he asked me to come along. At the time I was looking for Father so I told him I'd think about it, but now, it looks like Father's dead or stuck in some kind of a labor camp. We can't just wait around until they seal the thirty-eighth parallel . . . so I've decided to get out while I can."

Hun knew that it was becoming increasingly difficult to cross the thirty-eighth parallel, especially since land reform had been launched. That was why he felt as if his heart and the world around him were being split in two when Old Ko told him of the peasants' assembly, although it was hardly unanticipated.

"My friend said he was leaving tonight. At nine o'clock. He and a bunch of his friends are taking a boat from the Koni Island ferry crossing below Man'gyŏngdae Bluff. I can't make it tonight because I have to take Mother over to her brother's house. If only I'd taken her yesterday, instead of wasting my time asking for news of Father. I can hardly let her go by herself. She's been having dizzy spells ever since they took Father away. Besides, I have to tell Uncle where I'm going. I don't know what to do. Leaving with my friend tonight would have been the easiest way out . . . Myŏnggu and Pulch'ul must have escaped by boat too . . . So I was wondering, could you do me a favor?"

Hun nodded.

"Would you go to Pyongyang and ask my friend if he could postpone the trip for a day? If he can't, then ask him how I can get passage south later."

"Sure, I'll go right away."

"Thanks. Here's a map to his house." Hyŏk took a piece of paper from his vest pocket. "It's easy to find. You lived on the other side of town so you might not be familiar with this area, but all you have to do is head straight for

Kyŏngch'ang Gate from West Pyongyang Station and you'll come to the Sŏnman Rubber Factory on the left side of the road. Turn left at the factory, then right at the second alley on the right. His house is at the dead end. His name is Kim Shigŏl."

Hun took the map.

"Well, then I'll take Mother to Uncle's now." Hyŏk stood up. His face, which had grown noticeably thinner in the last few days, seemed to recover some of its color. "Why don't you leave on the boat with us?" Hyŏk asked.

Hun rose from his spot by the tomb. Actually, leaving for the South would settle things with Ojaknyŏ, if nothing else.

7

Hun caught the eleven o'clock train to Pyongyang. It was crowded. Hun had made three trips to Pyongyang since liberation, the first in late August, a fortnight after liberation; the second about twenty days later; and the last a fortnight after that. The train had been packed each time, so crowded, in fact, that people were riding on top of the cars, even on the cowcatcher.

It wasn't quite so crowded today. And the passengers were different this time. Back then most were returning to their homeland from Manchuria and other foreign places. There were country people too, anxious to see the newly liberated Pyongyang. Their faces were bright, full of excitement and emotion. And Hun had shared their feelings.

Today most of the passengers seemed to be tradespeople headed to Pyongyang on business. In the years immediately preceding liberation, these were the type of people who rode the train to Pyongyang. People who sat pondering and calculating. And the train was about as crowded as it was today.

Hun stood cramped in a corner, eyes on the window. The backs of his hands felt warm. A shaft of sunlight, pouring in through the paneless window, had sifted through the crowd to warm his hands. It shifted as the train changed direction and disappeared in the shadows of passing mountains, but it soon reappeared. At times it moved from Hun to linger just a few paces away or rest on the back of the passenger in front of him. Then Hun would stretch out his hands to warm them.

The sunlight reminded him of another trip to Pyongyang. An elderly couple were sitting side by side a few paces from where Hun stood, squeezed between the other passengers. They both looked to be a few years over ninety, and their white hair was cropped so short it was impossible to tell which was the husband and which the wife, except when the old man turned to reveal a straggly goatee.

The two began quarreling like small children. They were fighting over the rice cakes that a young woman, apparently their great-granddaughter, had given them. Each insisted that the other's was bigger. They switched pieces, but the bickering continued, and so they switched again. They started eating but it wasn't long before they were complaining that the red bean powder on the other's rice cake looked more delicious. They each took a bite of the other's rice cake. They carried on like a pair of foolish children. Perhaps it was true what they say about people returning to infancy in their old age.

The young woman simply gazed out of the window, seemingly accustomed to it all, but the other passengers gawked in delight as if watching a circus. The old couple ignored them, though. They were absorbed in their own world.

Not long after the rice cakes were gone the old man said he had to go to the toilet. The young woman told him to be patient. No doubt she meant to help him through the window at the next stop so he could relieve himself in the station yard. It would have been next to impossible to get to the lavatory at the end of the crowded car. Besides, Sŏp'o Station was only a few minutes away.

The old man kept badgering her, though. He simply

couldn't hold it any longer, he complained. The young woman gave up reasoning with him and rose from her seat. It was as if she were a mother pestered by her children. She helped the old man up and practically carried him through the crowd. They had almost reached the lavatory when the old woman let out a strange sound. Her voice was shrill, like a small child's. I have to go too, she cried. She had tears in her eyes. The old man called to her, beckoning with his hand, and the passengers passed the old woman down the aisle like a parcel. She looked as light as a child too.

The old woman didn't need to use the lavatory, though. She simply stood by the door, trying to peek inside while her husband was using it. As if she was afraid he might disappear when she wasn't watching.

The passengers said that the old couple had been acting this way from the moment they boarded the train in Chŏngju. At first they had been seated separately, but they made such a fuss, waving and calling to each other, that the passenger sitting next to the old man offered his seat to the old woman. It seemed that the old couple had just returned to Korea after living in Manchuria. They had spent a few days with relatives in Chŏngju and were now on their way to their eldest great-grandson's home in Sariwŏn. The passengers around them all agreed that the old couple would have to die together and be buried together or there would be hell to pay.

After their trip to the lavatory, the old man and woman were quiet, but it wasn't long before the quarreling resumed. This time they argued over who had the sunnier seat. It was early October and a chilly wind blew in the mornings and evenings. Their great-granddaughter made them exchange seats from time to time, and when it came their turn to sit in the sun, they folded their hands on their lap and closed their eyes with the untainted bliss known only to children.

As Hun recalled that scene, as beautiful as any fairy tale, he thought the old couple must be enjoying this sunshine too, even if they had left this world to share a grave in some sunlit place.

Hun closed his eyes and let the sun soak into his skin. He couldn't enjoy it the way the old couple had, though. As the train drew closer to Pyongyang, he was growing increasingly concerned. Should he act on his cousin's suggestion and leave for the South? He had to decide quickly if he was going to ask for a place on the boat.

The train stopped at West Pyongyang Station and everyone got off. Apparently it didn't go any further, although Central Station was supposed to be the last stop. The passengers seemed more numerous now that they had poured out of the train.

Hun checked the timetable before leaving the station. There was a return train at 4:50 P.M.

The broad street leading to Kyŏngch'ang Gate was almost deserted except for the people from the train. The excitement that had pervaded the city after liberation seemed to have subsided.

Hun stopped at a bicycle repair shop beneath the railroad overpass to ask for directions to the rubber factory. The owner was chatting with a customer as he sanded the bicycle tube slung over his knee.

"That's the second one today."

"Dropping like flies, eh?"

"Yeah, the measles are murder on those kids. I saw at least five corpses yesterday."

"They say the Japs are weak in the gut. Why, even the grown-ups croak from a simple bout of dysentery!"

"Exactly. They're in bad shape. They had the good life for so long and now they have no food to eat or clothes to wear. Just think of them sleeping on those cold *tatami* floors with the measles making the rounds!"

He must be going to Sŏjangdae Cemetery, Hun thought as he watched a man pass with a bundle in his A-frame carrier. His clothes were patched and tattered, and he was wearing canvas shoes.

"It must be his kid, eh?"

"I guess so."

"But he doesn't look sad."

"I guess people stop feeling anything after a certain point. At first, they put the kids in tangerine boxes or apple crates, but now, like that man, they just wrap them in straw mats. They used to bury them, too, but nowadays they just dump them in a hole in the cemetery. I hear the dogs tear out the kids' guts and drag them through the streets."

"Eck," the other man winced. "I'm not eating dog this summer!"

The shop owner looked up at Hun, as if to ask what he wanted. Hun, suddenly aware that he had been eavesdropping for too long, stammered, "Oh, excuse me. I wondered . . . " Suddenly he couldn't remember the name of the rubber factory. "There's a . . . rubber factory around here, isn't there?"

"Well, if you mean the Sŏnman Rubber Factory, it's right over there," the man pointed across the street with his sandpaper.

I should have walked a bit further, Hun thought, then I wouldn't have seen that awful sight. The Japanese man trudged on, seemingly oblivious of the child's dead body in his carrier. Perhaps an even greater bitterness blinded him to the sorrow. What if he saw the dogs tearing his child to pieces? It seemed as if he would simply stand by and watch. A cold shiver ran down Hun's spine.

On his second trip to Pyongyang after liberation, Hun had seen a Japanese man begging a butcher for a lump of fat. Perhaps he had been deprived of his regular diet for so long he craved fat now. Hun hadn't pitied the man at the time; in fact, he had felt the Japanese deserved a taste of their own medicine, but he felt sorry for the Japanese man today. Perhaps that was why he had forgotten the name of the rubber factory.

Hun turned left at the rubber factory. It was clearly the right alley, but Hun took out the map his cousin had given him anyway, as if to dispel the thought of the Japanese man.

Strangely, none of the houses had nameplates. Hun recognized the house at a glance, though, and pushed the gate. It was barred from the inside. He looked up to find barbed wire running the length of the wall. On his way here, Hun had noticed that everyone had barbed wire on their walls and oil drums dangling in the spaces between houses. The drums must have been placed there so the residents could sound a warning of marauding "liberators"—that is, the Russian soldiers. What a pitiful defense! And did they really need to bar their gates in the middle of the day? The excitement of liberation may have been gone, but that didn't mean the city was at peace.

He rattled the gate. The house seemed empty. But the gate was barred from the inside. There must be someone there. He rattled the gate again, louder this time.

There was a noise inside, then Hun glimpsed a patch of white clothing through the crack in the gate. The figure in white did not come to the gate, though. He seemed to be watching.

"Does Mr. Kim Shigŏl live here?"

"Yes. Who are you?" The figure asked cautiously.

"I came to speak to Mr. Kim."

"He's not here right now. He went to the country, to his grandparents' house."

He must have left for Seoul already, Hun thought, but he had to know for sure, and to do that, he had to convince this man that he could be trusted.

"Pak Hyŏk sent me."

"Pak Hyŏk?" the man echoed.

"Yes, I have a message from him."

The man in white came to the gate and quietly removed the bar. He was a middle-aged gentleman with long side-whiskers. Hun assumed he was Kim Shigŏl's father. The man inspected Hun's face, then peered past him into the alley.

"How do you know Hyŏk?"

"He's my cousin. It's about the appointment your son made with him."

The man held the gate open and gestured Hun inside, then closed it quietly and slipped the bar back in place.

"Has your son left already?"

"No, not yet." The man lowered his voice. "He's at his aunt's house."

"I see."

"He asked me to send Hyŏk over there when he arrives. My sister-in-law's house is just over Changdae Pass."

Hun asked the man to draw a map on the back of the one Hyŏk had given him. The man went inside and returned with a pencil.

"It's easier to get there by Sung'in Avenue," the man explained as he motioned Hun to a seat on the veranda, "but if you're going to take the streetcar, get off at Shinch'angni and go up the road that runs past the old Kwangmyŏng Bookstore."

The house was on the other side of Changdae Pass, but it looked easy enough to find.

Hun passed Sach'ang Market on his way to the streetcar station. It was bustling with people, as if the entire city had gathered there to leave the streets empty. Hun noticed a woman poking a foreign soldier in the belly, hoping to interest him in her wares.

He boarded the streetcar at Peony Peak Station and got off at Shinch'angni. The road to Changdae Pass was long and steep. To the right of the road was a church whose walls stretched to the ridge; houses lined the road on the left until they gave way to the embankment below Sungdŏk Primary School.

Hun stopped for breath at the end of the houses. He wiped the perspiration from his forehead and turned to look down the hill. He had come a long way. There was another man pausing for breath halfway up the slope.

Hun stopped to rest again at the top of the hill. There were three roads down the other side: one, a continuation of the road he had taken up, leading to Sung'in Avenue; a second descending to the left; and a third to the right.

The three roads were not on his map. Hun decided to try the one leading to Sung'in Avenue. He headed down the road, then turned into the first alley on the right, but he couldn't find the house with the blue plank gate that the man had indicated on the map. He tried the next alley on the left, but there were no blue gates. He tried every alley to the left of the road until he reached Sung'in Avenue, but without success. It was obviously the wrong road, he concluded, and started up the hill again.

Halfway up, he turned into an alley on the left, on the

chance the map was wrong. And sure enough, there was a plank gate painted a faded blue. He checked the map, but it clearly showed the house on the other side of the road. Perhaps the young man's father had confused the directions. After all, he had said they always approached the house from the other side.

Hun had no choice but to ask. The walls were topped with barbed wire, and the gate was barred from inside like the other house. He rattled the gate, and after a few moments an older gentleman emerged from the house. This time, Hun thought it best to identify himself at once.

"Mr. . . . Pak . . . from . . . Sunan?" The man repeated in a loud and clear voice. He must have meant for someone inside to hear, and soon a young man emerged from the house. He was pale, as if he hadn't been outdoors for some time.

"Are you Hyŏk's cousin?" the young man asked quietly.

"Yes," answered Hun. The young man asked him in, then motioned to the older man to bar the gate. The young man took Hun to a small room, empty except for a quilt and a few books. "I've heard a lot about you from your cousin." His voice was calm and resolute.

"I came to tell you Hyŏk won't be able to join you this evening. He wanted me to ask if you could postpone your departure."

The young man thought for a moment. "How much longer would he need?"

"Anytime, except tonight."

The young man paused again. "Well then, let's do this. The boatman said . . . actually, the boatman is my cousin, on my mother's side. . . . Anyway, he said that the spring flood tide comes in three days. Apparently that's the best time to launch a boat at night. You see, the water starts to ebb at midnight and doesn't came back in until dawn. I insisted on leaving tonight because each passing day means more danger, but if Hyŏk can't make it, I'll postpone the trip until the flood tide. We can't wait any longer, though. The boat will have to leave before midnight, so he has to get there by half-past eleven. We'll leave from the Koni Island ferry crossing, as originally planned. With a fair wind, we'll pass Chinnamp'o in two days. During the day we can pretend we're fishing." He paused, and then, with a flash of his eyes, he added, "It'll be an adventure. We're putting our lives on the line."

"I'll tell my cousin. And . . . I'd like to ask you a favor."

"What is it?"

"Is there any extra space on the boat?"

"For you?"

"Yes. And one other person."

"Well, it's a small boat, so we're trying to limit the number. But I'll do my best."

"Thank you." Hun was surprised at himself. Until he knocked on this man's door, he couldn't decide whether to leave or not, and now he was asking for two seats, not one. The second was for Ojaknyŏ, of course. He hadn't planned it that way, and yet he couldn't help but feel that he had been harboring the idea for a long, long time.

"The boat will be ready on the night of the twenty-eighth. I'll see you then. And by the way . . ." the young man lowered his voice. "Don't come here. Go straight to the ferry crossing. A suspicious-looking man has been snooping around the neighborhood ever since Hyŏk left. That's why I came here. I'm going to move again after you leave. We can't be too careful. They're like spiders watching for prey. Lately I've trusted my life to this window." The young man glanced to the window that looked over the alley. "So tell Hyŏk not to come looking for me. Send him straight to the ferry crossing."

What had the young man in the dog-fur coat said? *From now on, you're not allowed to step beyond a mile radius of this village without our permission!* And here he was, in Pyongyang without a word to anyone. But then, the warning had been made before land reform was put into effect. Perhaps it didn't matter anymore. Still, his young host reminded him that he too was being watched.

As he left the house, Hun felt as if someone was watching him from around the corner of one of the houses. He dared not look, though. Suddenly he recalled the man he had seen pausing for breath on the hill earlier. Perhaps he was tailing him. Hun could not remember what the man looked like, though, much less what color clothes he wore.

He headed down to Sung'in Avenue and stopped at the corner to buy a pack of cigarettes and matches. He stuck a cigarette in his mouth, lit a match and held it, without lighting the cigarette, until it had burned to his fingers. He blew it out and lit another. Again he stood there holding the match as he watched the passersby. The cigarettes were simply a ruse, but soon he realized that his pursuer, if there really was one, wasn't likely to walk past him, and so he started walking again.

Hun stopped at a restaurant at the corner of Sung'in and Sŏmun Avenues and ordered a bowl of soup with rice. As he waited for his order, Hun noticed he was still holding the map. He went to the lavatory and threw it in the toilet.

Hun left the restaurant and cut behind the Cheil Cinema to emerge on a broad avenue crowded with people. It looked like a good place to linger until it was time to catch the train.

He noticed some people gathered in front of a billboard.

Hoping to pass the time, he joined the crowd, but when he saw what was posted, he turned and hurried away. It was a copy of the *Workers' Daily*. He recalled the article about him that had appeared in yesterday's edition. Someone in the crowd might recognize me, he thought as he slipped into a back alley.

He passed the provincial government office and strayed into a Japanese residential district. A portrait of Stalin hung over the gate of every house. Hun imagined the measles-stricken children dying of cold and malnutrition inside. Unlike the neighborhood near West Pyongyang Station, this was an exclusively Japanese district so there were bound to be more children dying here.

Shortly after liberation Hun had been walking here when an airplane flew overhead. The houses had been silent as tombs, but when the airplane passed, the occupants burst from their homes to collect the handbills it had dropped. The handbills promised to protect the rights and safety of the Japanese. Fear and uncertainty had replaced the pride and dignity on their faces. Hun felt as if he had witnessed a defeated nation that day.

Hun wondered what time it was. He had given his pocket watch to Tangson. I might as well go to the station and wait, he decided. As he turned the corner and headed toward the post office, he noticed a face reflected in a window, the pale face of a woman whose hair was just beginning to grow back after being shaved off.

Shortly after liberation, Hun had seen many Japanese women with shaven heads along the country roads near his home. One day he came upon a cluster of ragged Japanese squatting at the edge of a field munching on something. They stopped chewing when they saw him and averted their faces. As he walked past, Hun realized they were hiding stalks of raw millet in their laps. Some had blackened their faces with soot and wore towels around their shaven heads. They were all women trying to pass as men.

As he neared the post office, Hun noticed a woman walking a few paces ahead of him. She was wearing a neat Japanese outfit and walked with an air of confidence. Hun eyed her with interest, for she was the first such Japanese woman he had seen since Japan's surrender. She may have shaved her head before, but now her short hair was greased back neatly like a man's. And her lips were rouged. She had much smoother skin than the woman he had seen in the window earlier.

The woman approached a Russian soldier standing in front of a house. They exchanged a few words, as if settling on a price. The woman's attitude betrayed a slight uneasiness. She must be relatively new to the trade. But it wasn't long before she followed the man into the house.

A female Russian soldier was directing traffic at the intersection in front of the post office. She had large breasts and a ruddy complexion.

Hun boarded the streetcar bound for West Pyongyang Station. Once more he remembered that someone might be following him. He might even be on this streetcar. Hun could not bring himself to look around, though. He just stared out into the street.

Suddenly he felt as if he had forgotten something. Yes, he had forgotten to go to the footbridge over the Taedong River and look at the water. And this may well have been my last chance to see Peony Peak and Silk Roll Island,* he thought with regret.

As the streetcar passed police headquarters, Hun saw the

---

*Peony Peak and Silk Roll Island are the two most scenic places in Pyongyang.

ubiquitous portraits of Soviet leaders lined up in front of the fountain in the square. Stalin's portrait was much larger than the rest. Along the base of the portraits were huge letters that read: "Long live the great leader Stalin, benefactor and liberator of the lesser nations." The gold medals adorning the leaders' chests shone ominously in the sun.

The streetcar passed Hwashin Department Store next, and there, on the walls of the second story, were portraits of South Korea's leaders, ugly, distorted pictures with malicious curses scrawled beneath.

A Russian soldier boarded the streetcar at Shinch'angni. From his uniform, Hun assumed he was an officer of some rank. The man sitting next to the soldier commented on his wristwatch, and the soldier pushed up the sleeve of his uniform to reveal four watches, all indicating the correct time, 3:35.

The man sitting beside the soldier nodded vigorously and exclaimed "Harasho, Harasho!" *They're beautiful!* Hun marveled at four watches all telling the same time.

After waiting in the station for over an hour, Hun boarded the train. It was more crowded than the train he had ridden that morning. Apparently the passengers who had taken the early morning train into the city were also going back on this one. The car was full of bundles and bags stuffed with food and other purchases.

The evening sun slanted through the paneless windows. The sun shone on his face as the train lumbered along, but it lacked the warmth he had felt that morning.

The train passed through Sŏp'o Station and stopped in Kanli. Hun glanced out the window and flinched with surprise. His uncle was standing on the platform waiting to board the same car by the rear entrance. He looked terrible; his clothes were covered with soot and his face was filthy, but it was clearly his uncle.

Hun turned to look at the rear entrance, but there was no sign of his uncle. Maybe he couldn't push his way through the crowd. Hun couldn't wade through the passengers to the rear of the car either. He thought of slipping out through the window and running around to check, but the train began to move. All he could do was wait until they arrived in Sunan.

But when he got off in Sunan, there was still no sign of his uncle. Hun waited until the train pulled out, but his uncle was nowhere to be seen. Then he realized that there was no entrance on the side of the car where he thought he had seen him. It must have been a station employee checking something. He just looked like Hun's uncle.

Hun noticed a young man standing by the entrance to the toilets as he was leaving the station. When their eyes met, the young man looked away and disappeared around the corner. He looked familiar. Had he been following him that day? Hun had seen him before but couldn't remember where.

As he headed home, Hun tried to recall who the young man was, but to no avail. He was sure the young man was behind him, but he heard nothing. It seemed like some kind of illusion. Who knows? Maybe it was all an illusion. Maybe no one had been following him in Pyongyang either.

A truck was standing in front of the town people's committee office. It must have come from county headquarters or the provincial people's committee.

Only then did Hun realize that the young man he had seen at the station was one of the party operatives who had come to his house on the day of the peasants' assembly. So he *had* been followed that day!

Ojaknyŏ had spent the day worrying about Hun and his trip to Pyongyang. Why had he gone so suddenly? Was he looking for a place to live? Was he planning to move to

Pyongyang? She had gone up the mountain to pick shepherd's purse, Hun's favorite spring green, but spent most of her time staring vacantly into the sky.

She simply missed him. She had never missed him so much. He had said he'd be right back so he was sure to be back by sunset. Hyŏk must be expecting him back today for he had come to wait in his cousin's room. Still, Ojaknyŏ was anxious, as if she were waiting for Hun to return from a long journey, not a simple trip to Pyongyang.

Restless, she went around the back of the house to the well. She could see Hun coming around the bend from there. Eyes glued to the path, she took one of his clean shirts from the line and rinsed it again and again.

A magpie flew into the woods, a feather in its beak. And before long a human figure appeared. It was Hun. No one else could have told who it was from that distance, but Ojaknyŏ recognized him immediately.

She rose, despite herself, and at a loss for something better to do, dropped the bucket into the well. Only after she had drawn a bucket of water did she look up and pretend to see him for the first time. She meant to greet him cheerfully, but couldn't.

"Your cousin's waiting for you," she said instead, her ears tingling with embarrassment. She lowered her head and went into the kitchen to prepare dinner.

She couldn't help overhearing the two men's conversation as she worked. She chided herself for eavesdropping, but couldn't keep her ear from the door.

"So did you see my friend?"

"Yes. Everything's settled."

"Is he going to postpone the trip?"

"Yes. He said to come to the Koni Island ferry crossing by eleven thirty P.M. on the twenty-eighth."

"Why so late? We were supposed to meet at nine thirty today."

"He said the spring flood tide begins to ebb at midnight that day, so everybody has to be there by eleven thirty. With a fair wind the boat will pass Chinnamp'o in two days, he said."

"Well then, I'll have to get to Pyongyang by afternoon."

"Yes, and he said you're not to come to his house. Go straight to Koni Island. Apparently someone's been watching him. He's been staying with his aunt for the last couple of days, and he said he was going to stay somewhere else after I left. You know, I think I was followed today, too. If I were you, I'd leave here at dawn so no one saw me."

"You're probably right. They're a bunch of vipers. But what about you? Are you coming with us?"

Ojaknyŏ leaned closer to the door, her heart pounding.

"Yes, I asked him to make room for me too."

"That was smart."

Ojaknyŏ's head spun. She felt as if her body were melting into the floor and she nearly fell on the dinner tray she was preparing. The steam from the shepherd's purse soup glimmered dizzyingly before her eyes.

Hun didn't tell his cousin that he had asked for two places on the boat. He'd find out soon enough. He considered telling him that he had seen a man who looked like his uncle at Kanli Station, but he didn't. There was no need to upset his cousin.

Son Yongp'al went out as soon as he finished dinner. He had a meeting to go to. Lately, not a day went by without some kind of meeting. Morning, noon and night, there were meetings, meetings, meetings, but tonight's gathering was important. Tonight they were making the final decision on land allocations.

And Yongp'al was dissatisfied with the way the land was being divided. The problem was Yukson, his thirteen-year-old son; the boy was counted as a child, although he did the work of a grown-up. Yongp'al had never heard of anything so unfair. It wasn't as if they were going to increase his family allocation in a few years when Yukson grew up. So Yongp'al had decided to demand a larger share for his son at the meeting that night.

But as he stepped down onto the stoop, Yongp'al froze. He saw something move in the direction of his former landlord's house. The stone wall separating the two houses was quite low, and in the opaque shadows beyond, he saw a man untying a horse in the stable. As the man turned to lead the horse from the stable, Yongp'al could see his face and clothes were as black as any chimney sweep's.

Yongp'al gulped back a scream and scurried into his house. "It's Yongje's ghost! He's come back! His ghost has come back!"

Yongje stroked the horse's neck as he led it through the yard. The horse recognized its old master and whinnied with delight. When he reached the gate, Yongje mounted the barebacked animal and spurred it in the flanks. He could feel the animal's warmth through his clothes. It had been a long time since he had felt such warmth.

He passed someone at the crossroads. It was Tŏsop. He was headed for Karakkol on orders from headquarters. A truck had come from Pyongyang to capture Pak Yongje, who had escaped from wherever they had sent him. Tŏsop was responsible for mobilizing members of the local youth committee and capturing Yongje if he showed up at his house.

Tŏsop didn't realize who the man on horseback was at first, not so much because of the darkness as because the rider's face and clothes were covered with soot. Then suddenly he realized that there was only one horse in the village and Yongje was the only one who knew how to ride.

"I'm in hot water if I don't get him," Tŏsop gasped. He turned and ran toward people's committee headquarters.

Yongje felt like a different person now that he was back on his horse. He felt as if he had finally reclaimed the self he had lost the day they dragged him away. What a terrible price he had paid!

They had taken him to the Sadong Coal Mine on the day of the peasants' assembly. He had been assigned the job of carting coal, rather than the actual mining, in consideration of his age, but the twelve-hour night shifts were more than he could bear. When the pain in his legs prevented him from working, his meals were withheld, on the principle that those who did not work should not eat. He had to push the cart if he wanted the three lumps of rice that made up his daily ration. The mine supervisors declared that the former landlords should experience first-hand the life of a laborer under the old system.

But for Yongje, it wasn't labor so much as penal servitude. And servitude with no end to his sentence! He was sure he would die there, without anyone knowing. And what had become of his family? He despaired of ever seeing them again. Yongje had one final wish. He wanted to see the unfinished reservoir. Yongje didn't understand this obsession himself, and yet he would have gladly exchanged his life for one last glimpse of the reservoir, though he knew he would never finish it now. It was clear he would not survive many more days in the mine, so he decided to escape, even at the risk of his life.

Yongje took off the following morning. As he emerged from the mine, he pretended to go to the outhouse but slipped out the gate instead. He headed straight for Mirim where a ferry crossed the river.

When he arrived at the crossing, he saw a boatman sitting in the stern of his boat, mending his net. Yongje approached him, but the man simply glanced at him, then turned back to his work. Yongje dug through his pockets but he had nothing. He took off his vest, placed it on the gunwale, and asked for a ride across the river.

The boatman glanced at Yongje once more, rose without a word, and picked up his oar. As he sat with his back to the brisk river wind, Yongje trembled lest the boatman ask him where he was coming from or in what direction he was going. Never in his life had he so dreaded talking with another man. Fortunately, the boatman didn't ask any questions, and when Yongje stepped from the boat on the other shore, the boatman told him to take his vest. Yongje begged him to keep it, but the boatman said he could pay on his way back.

"I won't be coming back," Yongje answered.

The boatman seemed to know that already. Another man had escaped from the mine the day before but he had already been captured.

"I wasn't going to give you a ride at first but I took pity on you because of your age. Just make sure you don't tell anybody I helped you!" the man said as he tossed the vest from the boat.

Yongje knew of the other escapee. A middle-aged man from Chunghwa County had fled the mine the previous day, but he had been recaptured and savagely tortured. I'd have died in the mine anyway, Yongje thought. Might as well take my chances.

He passed Mt. Chuam and cut in the direction of Sŏp'o before reaching Hŭngbu. He stayed on the mountain roads to avoid detection.

His legs were tired as he neared Sŏp'o, and his stomach ached with hunger. When he reached Kanli, the sun was waning and he knew he couldn't walk any further. He decided to hide in the station and sneak on the evening train.

It wasn't long before the train came in. He climbed onto the ledge opposite the entrance to one of the cars and clung to the handrail until the train pulled into Sunan Station. There he jumped from the train and hid until the train left, then looped around the dike to the east and headed home. Never in his life had he so feared the eyes of others.

Fortunately it was suppertime and there was no one around. He felt like a burglar as he climbed over the rear wall of his own house. After glancing around the inner quarters, which were empty as he had expected, he went straight to the stable. When he saw his horse standing in its stall as if nothing had happened, he forgot everything. His hunger and fatigue disappeared. All he could think of was riding to the reservoir.

Yongje's gray hair, black with coal dust in the evening light, fluttered in the wind as they galloped across the fields. The clatter of the horse's hooves echoed in the silence.

They soon reached the reservoir, and the horse stopped at the base of the dike before Yongje had a chance to pull in the reins. It seemed to know where its master wanted to go.

Yongje dismounted and climbed the dike. The water gleamed white in the twilight. Yongje felt his eyes tingle. It was as if a precious spark, dormant and forgotten for so long, had been rekindled. The image of the reservoir brimming with water rose before him. Now all I have to do is build the floodgate, yes, the floodgate, just the floodgate, he whispered.

A figure emerged from the darkness. It was Ch'ŏn Ondal, returning from his cotton field over the pass where he had spent the day spreading manure. He mistook Yongje for one of his neighbors. "Hu-Hu-who's there?" he asked.

When he heard no answer, he drew nearer.

"I—i-i-is that you, Kwa-wa-wanho? What are you do-o-oing here?"

As soon as he realized it wasn't Kwanho or anyone else from the village, he turned and hurried in the direction of home.

He ran into his neighbor Pang Handol at the entrance to the village. "Whe-whe-where are you going?" he asked.

"I heard a horse gallop by, so I came out to see who it was."

"You know wh-wh-what? It's a gho-o-ost! Old Yo-o-ongje's ghost! It wa-wa-was riding his ho-ho-horse!"

A pair of lights appeared in the distance and began bobbing toward them. Something weird's about to happen, the two men thought as they fled into the village.

The road to Chin'gol was crooked and uneven as it branched off from the main road to Hanch'ŏn. The truck bounced along slowly. Its headlights rounded the bend and shone on the reservoir, first illuminating the horse, then Yongje's back as he stood on the edge of the dike. The horse stretched its neck and let out a long whinny as the lights approached.

The truck halted at the base of the dike and disgorged several men. Tŏsop was among them.

Yongje stood motionless, staring down at the reservoir. Only when the men drew close enough to grab his arms did he move to shake them off and walk slowly down the inner wall of the dike toward the water. He must be mad, they thought.

He stooped to the water and washed his face and hands. Then, after drying his face on his shirt, he walked up the dike as slowly as before.

On his way to the truck, he ran his hand across the horse's back, and the animal shook its sweaty coat in reply.

The fields were pitch-dark by the time the truck began bouncing down the road again. Yongje felt as if he were racing into a coal mine tunnel, longer and deeper than any he'd seen before. It seemed endless as the headlights pierced the fathomless darkness.

They rode and rode, then suddenly the tunnel seemed to end in a wall. Yongje crashed against the wall. He couldn't tell if the wall had smashed into him or he had crashed into it, but he felt a wall tumbling down on him. It was like a concrete floodgate, the kind he was going to build at the reservoir, but this one was so high, it seemed to reach to the sky.

The truck screeched to a halt, and the men jumped out. Yongje was writhing on the ground. His head had struck the foundation of the old marble monument as he threw himself from the truck.

"Crazy old hoot! Didn't he realize he'd kill himself jumping out of a moving truck like that?"

Yongje's body was cold by the time Hun and Hyŏk arrived. Old Ko had told them of the accident. They carried the body to Hun's house and began mopping the blood from Yongje's head and shoulders. Soon their rags were covered with a sticky mixture of blood and coal dust.

As they changed the dead man's clothes, a shout echoed through the evening quiet. "To kill a serpent you have to smash its head!" Hun felt his hair stand on end. He knew who it was. He had heard the same shout a few days earlier when Tŏsop destroyed the monument.

Hyŏk paused to listen. He didn't recognize the voice at first. "To kill a serpent you have to smash its head!" the shout rang through the darkness once more.

"Is that Tŏsop?" Hyŏk's voice shook.

Hun remained silent.

"What's wrong with that man?" Hyŏk's face flushed with anger. He seemed ready to leap out the door. Hun grabbed his arm and motioned to the dead body with his eyes.

From the kitchen came Ojaknyŏ's suppressed sobs.

When they finished changing Yongje's clothes, Hun walked down to the crossroads in search of Ko. He wanted to ask the old man what they should do for a coffin.

Tangson stood in the crossroads holding a lantern as his grandfather spread ashes over the pool of blood left there.

"I was thinking of going straight to Sunan for a coffin," Hun said. "What do you think?"

The older man paused for a moment. "When's the funeral?"

"Tomorrow. As early as possible."

"Yes, you should get it over as soon as possible. I don't know about the coffin, though. When Grandma Bullye died, they went into Sunan for a coffin, but there weren't any, so they had to order one and go back and get it the next day. What if you go into Sunan and can't find a coffin or a coffin-maker? Then you won't be able to bury him tomorrow."

"So what should I do?"

"We could make one here if we had some wood."

"I have some boards at home. I was going to use them to build a loft over the kitchen."

"They're probably half-inch boards. Kind of thin for coffin boards. And narrow too."

"I don't know about my cousin, but we can hardly afford to be picky at a time like this."

"All right, then I'll ask Kang to go over to your house and make the coffin tonight."

Hun returned home, but the carpenter didn't come. A few hours later, Old Ko came with some tools. Kang must be coming later, Hun thought, but apparently that wasn't the case. "I swear the world must be coming to an end! Why, that Kang refused to make the coffin! His wife told me he was at a meeting, so I went and asked him to make the coffin, but he said he couldn't. Can't leave the meeting, he says, because they're deciding on the land allocations. So I asked him to come after the meeting, but he said he can't come then either. I ended up borrowing these tools from his wife. Figured I'd try and make the coffin myself. Can hardly blame him, though. It can't do him any good, being seen around this house, I mean."

Hun knew only too well what he meant.

He took the old man to Ojaknyŏ's room and began work on the coffin. Ko put on the glasses Hun had given him and studied the boards. He selected the boards with the fewest knots and began planing. Hun held the boards as the old man worked, but the plane kept catching and skipping. It wasn't simply because the old man was weak. Apparently, planing wasn't as easy as it looked.

Hun took a turn, but he was even worse at it than the old man. At this rate, they'd never finish the coffin by morning. Hun suggested they quit planing and start putting the coffin together. The old man refused, though. Can't let a dead body rub against a rough coffin, he said.

The door slid quietly open some time after the second crow of the cock. It was Kang, the carpenter.

"Thank goodness," Old Ko exclaimed.

Hun was relieved, too. Ko suggested he return to his room. Ojaknyŏ was sitting up with Hyŏk, but Hun was concerned about him.

Kang took out a plane from his belt as soon as Hun left the room. It was the one he had taken from Yongje's barn. The old man gave him a suspicious look, as if to ask where the plane came from, and the carpenter averted his eyes, muttering. "Don't think I'm here for old times' sake. I just came to try out this plane."

It could hardly be called a funeral. There was no bier, just a coffin wrapped in white cotton cloth.

Ojaknyŏ shortened the hemp mourning robe Hun had worn at his own father's funeral. Hyŏk wore it now, along with the mourning hat.Hun had worn. And Hyŏk and Hun were the only pall-bearers.

Old Ko and Ojaknyŏ preceded them to the grave site to dig the grave. Hun staggered under the weight of the coffin as they climbed the hill. They had to rest several times.

When they neared the grave site, someone jumped down from the flat spot by the graves. It was Samdŭk. He took Hun's end of the coffin. Hun was angry. He couldn't help thinking Samdŭk had come to spy on him, at his own uncle's funeral. He yielded his grip on the coffin, though, for he didn't have the strength to carry it any farther.

Samdŭk put the coffin down next to the grave, grabbed a hoe, and jumped back in the hole he had been digging earlier. "It'd have taken the whole day to dig that hole if it hadn't been for Samdŭk," Old Ko explained to Hyŏk and Hun. The old man then leaned over the hole. "You need to make it a little deeper, Samdŭk. The deeper the better."

Hun didn't like the idea of Samdŭk digging his uncle's grave. Samdŭk's A-frame carrier stood empty to one side of the hole. Ojaknyŏ must have put him to work after she caught him spying on them. Too bad they couldn't do it themselves, even if it would have taken all day. He turned with irritation to Ojaknyŏ. She was squatting with her back to him, collecting stones from the pile of earth next to the hole.

Samdŭk was the first to pick up the shovel after the coffin had been lowered into the grave. They could hardly allow Samdŭk to fill the hole, Hun thought. Hyŏk must have felt the same way, for he grabbed the shovel as soon as Samdŭk picked it up.

The grave was filled and a small mound made. All that remained was covering the mound with turf. Hyŏk said he would lay the turf himself and suggested the others go home. Hun in turn told Ko to go since the old man had stayed up most of the night. He insisted on helping with the turfing, though.

Hyŏk urged his cousin to take the old man home. The hard work was finished, he said, and he'd do the rest himself. Hun realized the old man wouldn't leave until he did, so he headed down the hill. Besides, his cousin might need some time to himself.

Samdŭk lingered by the grave until Hun and the old man left, then he shouldered his carrier and disappeared around the bend.

8

I have to go to my uncle's today. To let him know what happened to Father."

Hyŏk had returned late the night before. He must have cried a great deal after the others left. His eyes were red and swollen. He didn't seem to sleep well, either, though he must have been exhausted. A light sleeper, Hun had awakened several times during the night to find his cousin tossing beside him. In the morning, Hyŏk's eyes were even more bloodshot than the night before.

"I'm glad I took Mother to Uncle's house. Who knows what would have happened if she'd seen that."

Hyŏk stared straight ahead at the grove of trees in front of the old tomb. The branches quivered slightly, although there didn't seem to be any wind. Hyŏk was not looking at the trees, though; he was staring at something distant, something no one else could see.

Hun was looking at the field beyond the trees. A shimmering haze hovered over the rich brown earth. He hadn't noticed it the day before. And the poplar trees along the bank of the stream were wrapped in a cloud-like white vapor.

The trees by the tomb rustled, although the air seemed calm. Spring was making its entrance. It began with a breeze blowing down from the mountains, gradually reaching further and further until the earth thawed and haze rose from the fields to envelop the trees in mist. The breeze grew

milder with each passing day and finally it blew the flowers
open with its warmth. The sky seemed to be conspiring
with the earth to bring spring forth. Some days it sprinkled
rain quite out of the blue, then wrapped itself in clouds for
days without a drop of rain.

Hun turned to the cluster of pasqueflower shoots in front
of him. They were noticeably taller than the day before, and
the dark red buds were much fuller. He felt as if everything
around him was moving, changing.

He too would have to start moving. He had to leave this
place tomorrow at dawn. Tonight he would have to ask
Ojaknyŏ if she would come with him. He looked around the
grassy clearing. The old tomb had been his favorite haunt
for the past three years, but he may never see it again.

"You should go straight to the Koni Island ferry from
your uncle's," he said, "then you won't be followed. I'll
leave here tomorrow at dawn."

"All right. Be careful. I have to come back this way,
though. I have some unfinished business to take care of."

Hun looked up at his cousin. "I've been thinking," Hyŏk
said. "Yesterday at my father's grave and all last night. I
have to take care of something before I leave."

Hun sensed a desperate resolve in his cousin's voice.

"I mean Tosŏp, of course. I have to kill him . . . with my
own two hands."

Hun had hardly expected this, yet he could understand
how his cousin felt. Still, he had to dissuade him.

"Oh, he's just trying to survive. When you think about it,
he's a pretty pathetic old man."

"To survive? Does he have to become a devil to survive?
I don't care if he's chairman of the peasant committee. I
know, I used to hate anyone that had anything to do with
the communists, and when they closed the night school, I

thought we had to fight back, fire with fire. That's why I was glad Myŏnggu and Pulchul killed Kwŏn. But I've come to see it differently now. First of all, Kwŏn didn't do anything wrong. He was just a poor peasant. But Tosŏp's different. I think he wanted the post. Maybe he even asked for it. And even if he did do it simply to survive, why did he have to knock down the monument?"

"I suppose he was trying to prove that he'd broken all ties to his former landlord."

"All right, but why did he shout that stuff about serpents the other night? How could he say that when a man had just died?" Tears welled in Hyŏk's eyes. "I thought about it a lot yesterday at Father's grave, and later as I lay in bed. If it'd been someone else I might forgive him. But not Tosŏp. It's not simply because he owes so much to your family, but also because he and I share a very special relationship. You know, he saved my life when I was a child."

Hun had heard about the incident. It happened the summer Hyŏk turned eleven. There was a terrible flood, the worst in decades. The stream overflowed, creating a sea of water. Chickens and pigs were swept from their pens, but no one tried to catch them. By custom, a villager could claim anything he retrieved from the flood waters. During the summer rainy season, sturdy young men often dived in to collect logs, bundles of firewood, and livestock, both for the windfall and the chance to show off their bravery. However, no one dared to go in the water that day.

The villagers had gathered to watch the water when someone called out. "Look, a child!" Hyŏk had been swept up by the current as he was playing by the stream with some friends.

The villagers shouted excitedly, but no one jumped in, not even the young men who knew how to swim. Hyŏk was swept further and further downstream, but he didn't sink, perhaps because the current was so swift.

As Hyŏk drifted further from the crowd, Tosŏp plunged into the water. He'll never save the boy, the bystanders said. Hyŏk had already floated quite far downstream, but Tosŏp swam after him. He's going to drown too! gasped the villagers.

Hyŏk was swept into a muddy eddy and was struggling desperately to keep his head above water when Tosŏp reached him. The current was too strong, though. They're both going to drown! cried the people on shore.

Tosŏp finally managed to free the boy from the whirling eddy, but he seemed too tired to swim to shore. The frantic villagers dashed to the edge of the stream. He's going to drown if he doesn't let go of the boy!

Tosŏp and the boy finally reached land a good half-mile downstream. Tosŏp sprawled on the ground and passed out. There was a dark yellow cast to his skin for months after the incident. He looked as if he had survived some terrible illness.

"I owe him my life. I've appreciated that more and more as I grew older. If it weren't for him, I wouldn't be alive today." Hyŏk was staring at a point in space. "But look at him now. I know he used to bully your tenants in the old days, but I always figured they deserved it. I knew he was stubborn but I never thought of him as a bad man."

That was how Hun used to feel. He had been terrified of Tosŏp since middle school when he had seen him beating the tenant with the thresher, but after his father's funeral, where Tosŏp wept so bitterly, Hun decided he wasn't a bad fellow at heart.

"All right. Let's say Tosŏp took the job of peasant committee chairman to survive and knocked down the monument to prove he'd severed his ties with us. Still, how could he say what he did the other night? He's not human! Why, what he said was worse than any act of murder! I've thought long and hard on this. Who knows how much I've cried! I'm sad, but it's not like the sorrow I feel over the loss of my father."

Hyŏk paused to steady himself. "Tosŏp's gone crazy. There's no other way to look at it. Maybe he's not completely crazy, but he's getting there. There's no telling what he'll do. We have to get rid of him before he goes completely mad. That's the only way I can repay my debt to him."

Hyŏk kept staring at that spot in space. His eyes seemed fixed on a mental image he had planted there. Only then did Hun realize that he could not dissuade his cousin.

"I hid a dagger in the old chestnut tree. There's a hole." Hyŏk gestured to the tree towering above the rest of the grove. Then, fixing his eyes on the point in space again, he revealed his plan.

"I bought the dagger in Pyongyang, shortly after liberation, when there were all those rumors about the Japanese looting and killing people. And then the Russians started their troublemaking, so I figured I'd keep it handy. I nearly used it the other day when they came to get Father. I decided I'd kill that guy in the dog-fur coat and a few of his cronies if Father came to any harm.

"But I changed my mind after talking to my friend in Pyongyang. He said it's useless killing off a few lowly operatives. You have to destroy their organization with a force equal to theirs. But you know what? I have to kill Tosŏp. For his own sake.

"I'm going to ask him to come up here around five tomorrow afternoon. I'd like to get it over with right here and now, but I have to go to my uncle's today. Besides, I think it would be better to wait until after you're gone. You might not get out otherwise. So you make sure you leave at dawn tomorrow. I'll come back tomorrow afternoon, finish him off, and head for the ferry crossing after dark."

Hyŏk turned to Hun, as if demanding his promise, then rose. "I'll go see my uncle now. Be sure to leave at dawn tomorrow."

Hyŏk headed down the hill, but after a few paces he stopped. "A snake!" he shouted.

Hun sprang up in surprise. Were the snakes out already? It's only March! He dashed to his cousin's side, and there, in a patch of dry grass by the side of the path, was a black snake covered with red spots. It must have come out to sun itself, Hun thought, but it seemed listless, barely moving when they drew near.

"I hate snakes," Hyŏk muttered as he glanced around and picked up a stone. It was a piece of the marble monument, the fragment he had brought to show Hun a few days earlier.

Hyŏk smashed the snake with the stone. The animal squirmed, then blood began pouring from the gash on its back. Hyŏk picked up the stone again and sent it smashing down on the snake's head. The skull was squashed to a pulp.

"That's the end of him," Hyŏk muttered as he smashed the head once more. "It's true. You have to smash a snake's head to kill it."

A sound came from the direction of the Mountain Spirit Tree. It was Hŭngsu.

"What are you doing? Oh . . . a snake!" He reached down to pick up the carcass by its tail. "Why did you smash its head? It must have just come out of its hole. I bet it could hardly crawl yet. All you had to do was tie a string around its neck. What a pity! And this isn't an ordinary snake. It's poisonous—a real delicacy. I can tell by the tail. If only I'd gotten here earlier!"

Hun recalled what Ch'oe had said about Hŭngsu's fondness for snake meat.

Hŭngsu clucked in regret, then turned to Hun. "I've been looking for you. Ch'oe was killed last night in Sunan. Got shot in a drunken brawl, I guess. They say he took three bullets in the chest. Seems he picked a fight with a Russian soldier or something. I knew he was bound to get it sooner or later."

Hŭngsu turned his attention to the snake once more, muttering as he hurried on his way. "What a shame! This would have made a fine treat if it hadn't got squashed. Still, it's the first snake of the year. I'll have to have a barbecue!"

As he watched Hŭngsu disappear past the Mountain Spirit Tree, Hun thought of Ch'oe. The man had died believing he and Ojaknyŏ were lovers. It was not a total misunderstanding, he realized. After all, he was planning to flee south with her tomorrow at dawn. Hun felt a pang of guilt.

"Miserable piece of scum," Hyŏk grumbled as he watched Hŭngsu walk away. Then he turned back to Hun. "Be sure to leave tomorrow at dawn. I'll meet you at the ferry crossing at eleven thirty."

Hun stood watching his cousin until he disappeared around the bend at the crossroads. Suddenly he realized that this may be the last time he ever saw Hyŏk. His heart ached at the thought. Hyŏk was going to come back and kill Tosŏp at five tomorrow. That would give him enough time to reach the ferry crossing by eleven thirty, but what if he got caught!

All of a sudden Hun realized that *he* should finish Tosŏp

off, not Hyŏk. Yes, I have to do it. Me, and no one else.

Hun started down the hill. He paused when he reached the chestnut tree. There was a hole in the trunk about three feet off the ground. It was so dark inside it was hard to tell if anything was hidden there, but when he looked closer, he saw a steel blade propped against the side of the hole.

That's what I'll have to use on Tosŏp tomorrow, he murmured, as if he were making a pledge.

This would be his last night with Ojaknyŏ too. Now that he thought about it, Hun was glad he hadn't asked her to go south with him. How could he take back the invitation now?

He would have to say something tonight, though. He could thank her for looking after him all these years, if nothing else.

After supper, he lit the oil lamp and asked Ojaknyŏ to come to his room. She knew he was leaving. She had overheard his conversation with Hyŏk after he returned from Pyongyang and realized he had called her to say goodbye.

She gathered up his freshly washed underwear and stepped into the room, legs trembling with apprehension.

When he saw the pile of underwear, Hun said, "I just changed them the day before yesterday."

"Still, it's time you changed again . . . " Ojaknyŏ's voice shook.

I'll change my clothes for the last time tomorrow, Hun thought. As he looked across at Ojaknyŏ, he realized they hadn't sat face to face since the night of the land reform. Her skin had recovered its smooth texture after the fever's rash, but her face was pale as she looked at the floor, anticipating his final words of farewell.

His eyes dropped to the hands resting on her lap. They

were much rougher than he remembered, testimony to the three years she had served him.

Hun nearly blurted out a thank you for all she had done, but he stopped himself. He somehow felt that a verbal thanks would amount to an insult to the devotion with which she had cared for him for the last three years. Anything he said was sure to be inadequate.

Ojaknyŏ sensed his gaze and tucked her hands under her knees. She struggled to control her voice. "You must be careful not to skip meals, sir." She had been worried about his lack of appetite lately.

"It's not like I do any physical labor. I'm eating enough."

"And try to have soup with every meal."

It pained him to sit with her like this when she hadn't the slightest idea what would happen to him tomorrow.

"Ojaknyŏ!"

She looked up quietly, and yet her movement betrayed a certain alarm.

He didn't know what to say. He just looked into her eyes. Perhaps he had called her to his room so he could see those eyes one more time.

Ojaknyŏ could imagine what he was going to say. I have to hear him out, she thought, no matter what he says. She had to do at least that much. After all, it was the last chance she would ever have to help him. Still, a certain fear and sadness filled her eyes.

"Oh, did you hear what happened to your husband?" Hun asked, recalling what Hŭngsu had told him that morning.

A strange light flashed in Ojaknyŏ's eyes.

"I heard he was killed last night . . . Shot in a fight."

Ojaknyŏ closed her eyes and bowed her head.

"His family must be in terrible pain," Hun offered.

"Perhaps not. His parents may think it's better this way.

They gave up on him long ago. They've been living with
their second son." Ojaknyŏ was startled by her own words.
She was the one who wanted her husband dead, wasn't she?
Her heart pounded at the thought.

"He seemed like a decent fellow to me . . . so frank and
manly."

"It's true he's to be pitied in a way," Ojaknyŏ said. Then
she was startled at herself once more. After all, she was the
one to be pitied, wasn't she? Her eyes stung. She had
wished her husband dead out of concern for Mr. Pak, but
now he was leaving her.

"The world's so crazy, there's no telling who'll live one
day to the next," Hun reflected aloud. That was especially
true of him, and yet it didn't seem the least bit odd. He felt
calm, as if he could tell her anything. He actually felt he
could tell her what he planned to do tomorrow.

"Ojaknyŏ!"

She couldn't look up now. He's going to say goodbye,
she thought. She knew she had to hear him out, yet she
couldn't now. She wanted to savor this moment with Hun,
without thinking about what lay ahead. They could put off
their farewells until tomorrow, yes, until tomorrow.

"Ojaknyŏ!"

I have to look him straight in the eye, she thought, but
she heard a sound. "Oh, it's the cuckoo from Maiden
Rock!" she whispered.

Hun paused to listen.

It was the wind, gaining force after a lull in the early
evening. He couldn't hear the cuckoo.

"It'll sing again," Ojaknyŏ assured him, her eyes taking
on that dream-like gleam once more. "It sang last night, too.
Lately it's been singing every night. The rock will be covered with azaleas this spring."

Hun had a restless night, full of dreams.

He was standing on a vast empty plain. It was night, dark, without a single star.

An oxcart was jolting through the darkness, heading onto the plain. Squire Yun was sitting in the cart, one hand pressed to his forehead. It was strange. Hun could see everything despite the darkness.

A lantern was dangling from the rear of the cart. Hun hadn't noticed it before. It burned faintly in the darkness, and every time the cart hit a bump, the lantern swayed violently. It looked like it might fall off at any moment.

Hun shouted to Yun. "Your lantern's going to fall off!" But Yun simply sat there, his hand to his forehead. He didn't seem to hear.

Then the lantern called out. "Hold me! Hold me! I'm going to fall and break!"

Hun ran toward the cart. He easily overtook it, but it wasn't Yun riding on it. Who is that? he wondered. First it looked like his father, then his uncle. Hun looked more closely and realized it was himself.

The lantern had disappeared. He turned around and saw it shining from where he had first seen the cart. But it wasn't the lantern. It was Ojaknyŏ's eyes. Ah, those eyes! Yes, those eyes! They're what I've been searching for all along.

He ran to her and took her in his arms. "You're mine now! I want to sow my seed in your healthy flesh. I want to cleanse my cowardly blood in yours!"

But he wasn't holding Ojaknyŏ. It was Tosŏp, her father. He had just stabbed him in the heart with the dagger. Blood poured from the wound. But not only from Tosŏp's chest— it poured from Hun's heart as well. Soon his body was covered with blood. But he was not afraid. Let it flow! he thought. Drain me of this cowardly blood!

Even though he was dreaming, he recalled an incident from middle school. There had been a special lecture that day. A surgeon was speaking about a patient who needed emergency treatment because of a car accident or something. The patient was bleeding heavily, he explained, and continued to bleed throughout the operation.

Hun couldn't follow the lecture. He kept thinking about the bleeding. The man had bled from the moment of the accident all the way through the operation. How horrible! The next time the lecturer mentioned the bleeding, Hun cried out, "Stop, please stop the blood!" and fainted.

But now, he wasn't a bit frightened by the blood gushing over him. Let it flow! he thought, let it flow!

Soon he was standing in a sea of blood. There was blood everywhere. He began swimming, but he was pulled deeper and deeper into the sea. He came to an eddy bubbling with blood-red foam. He knew he would die if he was sucked into the eddy.

"Help! Help!" he screamed. He woke to the sound of his own voice. His body was covered with cold sweat.

When he dropped off to sleep again, he dreamed he had gone to the ferry crossing to catch the boat. The others had already boarded, Hyŏk and his friend from Pyongyang, they all were there. There was only one seat left. His cousin beckoned to him, but Hun was angry. "Why didn't you leave two spaces?" he yelled. He had never yelled so fiercely. He yelled and yelled until he woke once more at the noise.

He dropped off to sleep again. This time he had turned into a cuckoo. He sang out. Ojaknyŏ's eyes shone with a dreamy happiness at the sound. He sang and sang. If I keep singing like this, my throat might burst and kill me, he thought. Still he sang and sang.

9

Hun went to his ancestral graves early the next morning. As night fell, a strong wind had begun to blow, but it was quiet now. The air was still cold, as it is on mornings in early spring, but it was somehow soft and fresh as it brushed across his forehead and lifted his heavy spirits.

Only yesterday the dark red earth had borne the final traces of frost, but now it swelled with warmth and moisture. It wasn't uncommon for ice to linger in the dark mountain shadows until early April when the villagers weeded the grass around their family graves, but this year spring seemed to be arriving early.

There had been no birds last time he had visited the graves, but today they were hopping nimbly from tree to tree. They looked so light. Spring is here! he thought. As he walked toward the altar stone in front of his parents' tomb, Hun kept mistaking the birds' shadows for the birds themselves.

The sooty circle left from the fire he had lit to burn the land deeds was still visible on the altar stone. Will it remain until the stone is covered by moss and worn away by the wind and rain? The thought was as distasteful as a festering sore.

He took a photograph from his pocket. It was the one taken on his first birthday. He struck a match and touched it to the photograph. It vanished in a puff of smoke. There wasn't a trace of him left now. He felt clean and free.

On his way home, Hun stopped at the tavern. Pulch'ul's mother was rinsing rice in the kitchen. She looked up in surprise.

"What brings you here so early in the morning?"

"I've been to my parents' grave."

"Why? Isn't it a bit early for weeding?"

"Can I have a bowl of rice wine?"

"Sure. Why don't you go inside?"

"No, I'll just drink it here."

He drained the bowl in a single gulp. He hadn't eaten breakfast and the alcohol warmed him instantly. Still, he asked for another bowl. I'll take a long nap when I get home, he thought.

It was almost noon when he awoke. He had eaten a few bites of breakfast as soon as he returned home, then collapsed into bed and slept. His head felt much clearer now.

He had to say something to Ojaknyŏ. He hadn't told her anything the night before. He had tried but failed in the end. What could he say when she was so absorbed in the cuckoo's song?

He opened the door to the kitchen, but Ojaknyŏ wasn't there. She must be in her room or the backyard. It seemed silly to go looking for her since he would see her at lunch.

He took a few gulps of the scorched-rice tea that was sitting by his pillow and went outside. He didn't want to go to the old tomb. He was afraid that he might imagine what was going to take place there later that day. He headed toward the orchard instead. It seemed like a good place to while away the time.

It was still early for a stroll through the orchard. In winter, Hun walked to the old tomb, but when spring approached and the abandoned fruit trees surged with new buds, he went to the orchard instead. And in autumn, when the fruit trees shed their leaves and frost covered the ground, he returned to the old tomb.

He had known nothing of fruit trees until he came back to live in the village. He had always assumed that the buds, which later became leaves and flowers, formed in the spring. But he was wrong. The trees prepared new growth for the coming year before they shed their leaves in the fall. The fragile buds then endured the cold winter to develop into leaves and flowers in the spring. Hun had been amazed when he first discovered this. What a marvelous mystery!

Some of the trees had no leaves or flowers, though. They had died over the winter for lack of attention. Some even died in summer, covered with rich foliage. It was a pathetic sight.

The rest of the trees sprouted leaves and flowers in season. He had to be careful when he walked through the orchard in late spring, for the untended boughs hung low, heavy with blossoms. He often had to push back the branches as he walked, and when he released them, the bees would buzz in surprise and swarm about his face. And if there was a wasp among them he had to be especially careful.

When the blossoms began to fall, Hun was filled with a strange anticipation. Would there be much fruit this year? Most of the blossoms didn't bear fruit, though. Indeed, each year there seemed to be less and less, and the fruit that did form dropped before ripening. If any remained, they were promptly stolen by the village children as soon as they ripened.

Some of the fruit rotted right on the branches. They turned a sickly yellow, then darkened and shriveled. Some of this shriveled fruit clung to the branches long after the leaves had fallen. It was a pitiful sight, the shriveled fruit hanging against the high, blue autumn sky.

Hun counted the remaining fruit on his daily walks. One by one they fell in the wind. When the last had fallen, Hun would start walking to the old tomb on the hill behind the village instead.

They'll blossom again this spring, he thought, but the meager fruit will rot or fall unripened. A few more trees will die, and new plants and trees will grow in their place.

Hun parted the branches and walked toward the old bower. Actually, it wasn't a bower so much as the spot where a bower once stood. It had been quite lovely, built to provide refuge from the heat of the summer, but it had deteriorated from years of neglect after his uncle lost interest in the orchard, and finally collapsed during the summer rains last year. All that remained was the wooden floor, half rotten and forlorn. Hun had often rested there during his walks in the orchard, for as recently as last summer it still had a roof, albeit rotting, and wobbling pillars.

Whenever he stepped into the bower, he lifted his hand to brush aside the cobwebs, only to realize that they were not cobwebs but rays of sun shimmering through the rotten thatch roof. Still, he swung his arm in front of him whenever he stepped through the dilapidated arch.

The villagers sometimes came to the bower too, for it was cool even on the hottest day. One afternoon during his first summer back in the village, Hun found a man sitting alone there, his shirt open. A butterfly flew into the bower, as if it too was seeking refuge from the heat. It circled the bower, then alighted on the man's head, but he just sat there, seemingly unaware of the butterfly. And after a while, the butterfly took flight again.

Suddenly Hun wished the butterfly would land on his head. It flew from the bower, though, sketching a series of short arcs before it disappeared into the trees. At the time,

Hun had decided that he would live in the country until bees and butterflies alighted on him, but now he only wished the hours would pass quickly and end his life there.

Through the trees Hun caught a glimpse of Samdŭk heading up the mountain with an empty A-frame carrier on his back. I hope he doesn't show up later on, he thought.

Hun then heard a chirping sound. He hadn't noticed it before. He followed the sound and discovered a flock of chicks, chirping as they sat nestled in their mother's bosom. The dozing hen started at his footsteps and puffed up her feathers in defense.

Hun turned to walk away. The hen's instinctive response seemed to hint at what might take place between him and Tosŏp a few hours later.

He walked to the edge of the orchard. A wheat field stretched over the slope below. The bluish shoots bristled with life. At the foot of the slope was the road leading to the upper village and Hanch'ŏn, and beyond that, a plain shimmered with the warmth of spring. The glistening spring haze seemed more pronounced than yesterday.

Across the way a green mist enveloped the poplar trees on the banks of Dragon Head Stream. It, too, looked even greener than yesterday.

Suddenly Hun was struck by a thought. If someone on that distant plain was looking in this direction, they were sure to sec the spring haze and green mist floating over the orchard, and he too would be wrapped in the mist.

Somehow that thought made him feel like an intruder. He turned from the field. I don't belong here! I don't belong here anymore!

He didn't eat much lunch. He had to say something to Ojaknyŏ. Hun opened the door to the kitchen when the clinking of dishes stopped, but she wasn't there. She must have gone to her room. He thought of calling her to his room, but then he realized he had nothing worth saying. What could he say?

Perhaps he wanted nothing more than to see her eyes once more. At breakfast and lunch, she had kept her eyes on the tray as she entered his room. Perhaps that was why he wanted to see her now. He longed to see her eyes one last time.

Years earlier, Hun had yearned for one more look into her eyes before leaving. He was moving to Pyongyang with his family. The furniture and pots and pans had been sent by oxcart at dawn. Hun and his mother were to take the mid-morning train from Sunan.

The women from the village came to his house to bid farewell. Hun thought Ojaknyŏ would be among them. The night before she had said she would come to say goodbye in the morning. Her mother had come early, but Ojaknyŏ was nowhere to be seen.

Her house was quite close to his, and when Hun and his mother set out along the main road, he looked back toward her house several times. She did not come out, though.

The women turned back at the entrance to the village. There still was no sign of Ojaknyŏ. I should have gone to her house this morning, he thought.

As the train pulled out of Sunan Station, it began to rain. The sky had been threatening rain since morning. Hun stared out the window recalling what Ojaknyŏ had said the night before. "You're so lucky to get to live in Pyongyang." Her large eyes filled with tears as she looked at him. "What's so great about Pyongyang?" he murmured, as if in reply.

Throughout the journey, Hun's mother offered him hard-boiled eggs, but something made him refuse.

Today he had only to call Ojaknyŏ and she would come. But he couldn't. He was afraid the very sight of her would shake his resolve.

Ojaknyŏ dreaded Hun's farewell, too, and hurried to her room as soon as she finished the dishes. She had resigned herself to his departure, but feared she wouldn't be able to say farewell without crying. I can't cry today, she thought. Years ago when Hun left with his family for Pyongyang, Ojaknyŏ hadn't gone out to say goodbye because she knew, even as a child, that she would burst out crying. She had gone to the hill overlooking the road to Sunan instead and cried when he disappeared from sight. She stood in the rain crying until the train vanished around the bend. Only later did she realize she had bitten a hole right through the sash on her dress as she cried. She thought of Hun whenever she saw the hole, and soon began to identify with the girl in the legend of Maiden Rock.

She was much luckier, of course, for she had lived to see Hun's return while the maiden in the legend turned to stone before her lover came back to the village. Why, she had even lived under the same roof with him for three years! In those years she had savored the happiness of a lifetime. It was much more than she deserved. She could die without a single regret.

Ojaknyŏ had already decided where she would go after Hun left. The cliff near Maiden Rock.

Hun left the house without a word and headed for the crossroads. Old Ko was threshing straw in his front yard.

Hun asked Tangson what time it was. The boy scampered inside and returned with the watch. "It's a few minutes past three," he said, holding out the watch for Hun to see.

He still had lots of time.

"Why don't you take the watch back?" Ko paused from his work. "People like us don't need to tell time."

"That's all right. I don't need it either," Hun said. Soon he would have no need to tell the time.

"Well, the boy's awfully fond of it. He doesn't wear it, for fear of breaking it. He's hung it on a hook in the room. Looks at it a dozen times a day. . . . Won't even let me get near it!"

"It looks like the watch has found its rightful owner."

Tangson ran inside to put the watch back, lest his grandfather insist he return it to Hun.

"See what I mean!" The old man chuckled, then spat on his palm and took up the thresher once more. "It's been a dry spring, and that halo around the sun is a sure sign of drought," he muttered. "In troubled times like this, we need a good harvest," he added as he brought the thresher down on the straw.

It was still too early to go looking for Tosǒp, so Hun decided to burn the straw for the old man. He gathered up an armful and started a fire in one corner of the yard. Then he poked a hole in the bottom of the burning straw with a long stick and began blowing in it. When one armful was nearly gone, he brought another, then another.

Hun noticed a peculiar red glow at the center of the fire. It was empty husks of rice. Each hollow kernel was glowing a brilliant red, brighter than the surrounding stalks of straw.

Hun recalled the old man's words—in troubled times like these. He too lived in a troubled time, and soon he would burn like those empty husks. He wanted nothing more than to burn with that beautiful red glow.

A handful of villagers appeared on the road from Sunan.

"Was there another meeting today?"

"When isn't there? Why, they have meetings morning, noon and night nowadays. I hear they are having another one of those peasants' assemblies today."

Tosŏp should be back soon, Hun thought as he rose to go.

"When are you going to finish this threshing?" he asked.

"Looks like it'll take till evening."

"Then, would you give this note to my cousin?" Hun had written it after Hyŏk left the previous morning. "He'll be passing this way around five."

The sole purpose of the peasants' assembly that day was to remove Tosŏp from his post as chairman of the peasants' committee.

The party had no further use for him. He had been selected because he was the estate agent for the largest landowner in the area and the party felt he was the best man to set the peasants against the landlords. But now that land reform was complete, he was useless.

In the early days of the new government, the party implemented such decisions on its own, but now it convened peasants' assemblies to make all party decisions seem like spontaneous exercises of the people's will.

The ostensible reason for Tosŏp's purge was his exploitation of the local peasants during his years as a running dog for the reactionary landlord prior to liberation. Of course, no one knew why this hadn't been considered when he was first appointed. He was also accused of maintaining close ties to the landlords. The fact that he had sent his son Samdŭk to help with the burial of the reactionary landlord Pak Yongje was offered as proof of the charge. Hŭngsu was appointed to replace him.

Tosŏp felt as if the sky had fallen. How can they do this to me? They promised to overlook my past if I cooperated. And I've done everything they ordered me to do. Why, I've done more than they've asked! And is this my reward?

Tosŏp's burnished jaw trembled slightly.

"Samdŭk!" he bellowed as he stepped through the front gate.

"He went up to gather firewood a little while ago," his wife answered in a timid voice. "He'll be right back," she added cautiously.

"Damn!" Tosŏp growled as he stalked into the shed. He brought out a sickle and began sharpening it on the whetstone in the yard. "You just wait till that brat gets here! Just wait!" His hand shook as he ran his finger along the blade. He couldn't tell if the blade was sharp enough. "Just you wait! Why did the son of a bitch go to Yongje's funeral? I'll hack the little bastard's head off!"

Then suddenly Tosŏp realized something. Someone must have squealed about seeing Samdŭk at Yongje's grave. Who could it have been? He paused from his work for a moment. It must have been Hŭngsu. Yes, Hŭngsu snitched so he could get the chairman's job.

Tosŏp felt like taking his sickle to everyone who had crossed him. Only then would he be satisfied.

Hun arrived while Tosŏp was still at the whetstone. Tosŏp turned at the approaching footsteps and sprang to his feet.

"I'd like to have a word with you." Hun announced, voice trembling.

Tosŏp's eyebrows twitched. Yes, let's have it out right here and now. It's all your fault. You're the reason I'm in this mess! I don't know why you're here, but let's settle the score once and for all.

Tosŏp tightened his grip on the sickle as he stepped toward Hun.

"I'd like to speak to you in private," Hun said and started up the hill.

Tosŏp coughed noisily and spat to the side of the path as he followed Hun. Every time Tosŏp spat, Hun felt as if the sickle blade was piercing his back. His hair stood on end, and yet he somehow managed to remain calm.

They entered the grove of trees by the old tomb and stopped next to the chestnut tree. All Hun had to do was take the dagger from the hole and stab Tosŏp. He hadn't planned how or where he was going to do it, though, and now Tosŏp had a sickle.

If only Tosŏp would stab him with the sickle first. Quite unconsciously, Hun slipped his hand in his pocket and pulled out the pack of cigarettes he had bought in Pyongyang a few days earlier. He struck a match, but it went out before he could light his cigarette. Hand shaking and breathing unevenly, he struck another match, but it went out too.

Tosŏp stepped past him and paused to fill his pipe. His sickle under his arm and his back to Hun, he struck a match and took a long draw. I'll never be able to kill this man, Hun thought. Tosŏp may be older but he's big and strong. I'll be the one killed.

Suddenly Hun realized that he may have brought Tosŏp here not to kill him but to be killed by him.

The thought gave him strength. He took the dagger from the hole and threw himself at Tosŏp's broad back with a shout.

Tosŏp spun around and the pipe dropped from his mouth. The dagger had sliced his right side. The instant Hun felt it cut Tosŏp's flesh, he let go of the handle and tumbled forward.

Tosŏp was stunned at first. He stared blankly at Hun, then reached for his side as if he had only then realized he had been stabbed. The blood was soaking into his clothes.

Tosŏp raised his sickle into the air. He was gasping for breath. Hun felt dizzy as he stared at the bloody wound. It wasn't like his dream the night before.

Tosŏp advanced toward him, one step, then another, the sickle still raised. Hun closed his eyes.

Then he heard a sound. A thud, as if a bundle of sticks had fallen on the ground.

"Father!" a familiar voice rang out.

Hun opened his eyes.

It was Samdŭk. He had thrown himself in front of his father and grabbed the hand that held the sickle. The tip of the blade had pierced his left shoulder.

"I've been waiting for you!" Tosŏp bellowed. "I'll finish you off first!"

Tosŏp leaned into the blade, but Samdŭk wrapped his hands around his father's arm and twisted. Tosŏp's arm rose higher and higher until he staggered backward and fell. Samdŭk tumbled on top of him.

Father and son wrestled on the ground, the blood from their wounds soaking each other's clothes. After a desperate struggle, Samdŭk wrenched the sickle from his father's hand and hurled it away.

Tosŏp sprang up, searching for another weapon. Finding nothing, he flopped to the ground with a low-pitched groan.

Tosŏp could feel the strength draining from his body. Perhaps it would have been better to die at Hun's hand, he thought. He heaved a sigh and slumped forward. Then, as if prompted by a sudden thought, he took some tobacco from his pouch and pressed it on his wound. He then tossed the pouch to his son. You can't give up, he seemed to say.

Samdŭk pressed a handful of tobacco into the wound on his shoulder and walked over to Hun. His whole body was shaking.

Hun shuddered too, his teeth rattling uncontrollably.

"I was afraid something like this would happen," Samdŭk said in a husky voice. "That's why I've been following you. Today I came up to gather firewood 'cause I saw you in the orchard. Who'd have known. . . . "

Hun felt dizzy for a moment. Had Samdŭk been trying to protect him? Was that why he was following him?

"I wanted to tell you to leave the village, but I felt sorry for my sister." Samdŭk paused. He seemed to have come to a difficult decision. "But now you have to leave. At once. You mustn't be smeared with blood again." His eyes filled with tears. "And please, take my poor sister with you."

Hun looked up at the young man, but he couldn't see a thing. A spark was burning within him. "What are you waiting for? Go to her! Go to Ojaknyŏ!" it seemed to say.

Hun took a deep breath and started running toward home.

Old Ko had nearly finished winnowing the straw when he saw Hyŏk dart past his house. The old man recalled Hun's note and called out. "Your cousin asked me to give you this," he said as he handed Hyŏk the note.

Hyŏk's face was flushed as he unfolded it. He read the simple message in the light of the setting sun: "I'll take care of Tosŏp. Go straight to the ferry crossing. Let's not have any more bloodshed."

Suh Ji-moon is professor of English at Korea University in Seoul. She received her Ph.D. from the State University of New York at Albany. Her translations from Korean include *The Rainy Spell and Other Korean Stories* (1983, revised and expanded edition, 1997) and stories by Hwang Sun-wŏn included in the 1989 collection *The Book of Masks*.

Julie Pickering is a freelance translator and editor living in Seattle.